BEHIND THE SEX OF GOD
Toward a New Consciousness—Transcending
Matriarchy and Patriarchy

BEHIND
THE SEX
OF GOD

Toward a New Consciousness—
Transcending Matriarchy
and Patriarchy

CAROL OCHS

Beacon Press   Boston

Copyright © 1977 by Carol Ochs

Beacon Press books are published under the auspices
of the Unitarian Universalist Association

Published simultaneously in Canada by
Fitzhenry & Whiteside Ltd., Toronto

Printed in the United States of America

(hardcover) 9 8 7 6 5 4 3 2 1

The symbol used on the title page is taken from
The Book of Signs, by Rudolf Koch
(New York: Dover Publications, Inc., 1955).

Library of Congress Cataloging in Publication Data

Ochs, Carol.
    Behind the sex of God.
    Bibliography: p.
    Includes index.
    1. Sex and religion.   2. Sex (Theology)
I. Title.
BL65.S4025   231   76–48519
ISBN 0–8070–1112–6

Dedicated to

Herman Blumenthal

and Clara Michaels Blumenthal

ACKNOWLEDGMENTS

I would like to give thanks to my students at Simmons College, whose interest and enthusiasm encouraged my research; to the Simmons Fund for Research, which gave me the seed money to begin this book; and, most of all, to Michael Ochs, whose translations, stylistic and substantive criticisms, and untiring bibliographic aid have done so much for this book.

CONTENTS

In the Beginning

THE MAJOR concern of this book is to show how
the dichotomy of matriarchy and patriarchy has affected
religious thought. It began as an intellectual adventure, an
attempt to discover a consistent pattern in seemingly unrelated Biblical stories and injunctions. I became convinced
that there was a logic that related the form of creation to
the destiny of the creatures; the concept of God to the concept of sacrifice. I was also aware that my expectations
were different when considering Greek stories and Biblical
stories and when considering the Olympian religion and
the Eleusinian mystery religion. In the beginning I was
simply lining up concepts. I had no preconceived idea of
which concepts would belong where or even what distinctions I was drawing out. Little by little it became clear that
the Judaeo-Christian tradition which represented patriarchy, although not in its pure (probably never realized)
form, gave to the concepts of patriarchy overriding significance. The Eleusinian mystery religion, one of the major
religions in Greece for a period of almost two thousand
years, was matriarchal and gave similar importance to matriarchal concepts. As I began to draw out the distinctions,
I saw them line themselves up not only as distinct from
one another but in opposition. It now became necessary to

test my perceptions against those of others. For this purpose I used several approaches: a Jungian approach (Neumann, Kerényi, Harding, Jung); an anthropological approach
(Bachofen, Briffault, Frazer, Lévi-Strauss, Douglas); a
comparative religion approach (Eliade, Hooke, Harrelson,
Harrison); an archeological approach (Patai, Mylonas, Albright, Gordon); a psychological approach (Bakan, Freud,
Jung, Fromm); and a philosophical approach (Spinoza,
Kant, Cassirer, Langer, Daly).[1] I found that we have certain
patterns of thought, ways of structuring and understanding
the many perceptions that constantly bombard us. These
are necessary or the myriad sense data will overwhelm us,
leaving us disoriented. It is *not* necessary that these patterns be unconsciously adopted, unscrutinized, the archaic
inheritance of a less self-conscious age.

I focused on one pattern—the pattern based on the opposition of matriarchy and patriarchy. It is far more pervasive,
deep-rooted, and influential than generally acknowledged.
As the constellation of concepts and values that belong to
this pattern of thought is drawn out, we will see it influ-
ences every aspect of human life. It affects the grounding
of our ethical code, our view of the material world, our concept of the meaning in or of life, and our attitude toward
death.

What I wish to accomplish through this book is fivefold:
(1) I want to point out that there are different modes of
religious thought. I will specifically examine three—matriarchal, patriarchal, and androgynous—and then present a
personal monistic position. (2) I want to show how deeply
interconnected these modes of religion are to our views of

reality. In part this is true by definition, if we accept the definition that religion is the way we center our lives—that is, our source of meaning and value. But even if we accepted a more restricted notion of religion, our view of the creation and our place in it informs our view of the world which surrounds us and of which we are a part. (3) I want to make the patriarchal view explicit, thereby making conscious a value system unconsciously absorbed in Western society: It is to make us conscious of why we may be uncomfortable with our bodies and the various transformations they undergo; to explain the curious antagonism in Western society toward certain concepts such as left-handedness, night, and odd numbers; and to force us to scrutinize our feelings about the material world and our own material existence. (4) I want to show the matriarchal alternative to the patriarchal mode of thought. Matriarchy is examined because it has not been seriously considered in the Western tradition. Understanding it is necessary to make sense of certain aspects of patriarchy. (5) Finally, I want to go beyond the two alternatives. They are worked out in opposition to one another and each responds to only one part of our felt needs and lived experience. I will suggest that the opposition of matriarchy and patriarchy can be overcome not by opting for one rather than the other, nor even by combining the two. I will suggest that the apparent duality can be transcended and a genuine unity achieved.

My approach is to begin with an examination of the concept of creation ("The Frankenstein Motif") and its implications for ethics. This is followed by a study of a predominantly matriarchal system, the Eleusinian mystery religion. We will see how it differs from patriarchal counterparts and what could be considered its strengths and weaknesses. Next, a patriarchal world view is examined through a consideration of the sacrifice of Isaac, a story central to the entire Judaeo-Christian tradition. Many philosophers and theologians have tried to understand this key story but their explanations have, for the most part, left still more unanswered questions. Within the context of the conflict of matriarchy and patriarchy, however, the story makes sense.

The chapter "Wandering" applies the logic of patriarchy to the stories of Cain, the Tower of Babel, and the emphasis on exile. But since no religion is purely patriarchal, some matriarchal elements persisted and others were reintroduced into the Judaeo-Christian tradition. This is shown in the next two chapters. "The Feminization of Judaism in the Zohar" deals specifically with the elements opposed by patriarchy. "The Cult of Mary" is concerned not with the historical Mary, but with how the concept of Mary functions in theology.

In "The Characteristics of Matriarchal Religions," the opposing categories in matriarchy and patriarchy are drawn out. This was the original material that excited my curiosity and led to the constellation of categories. I discuss eleven categories of opposition: five essential ones and six I call "secondary characteristics." There are many more and it might be the start of the reader's own adventure to take a practice previously unquestioned and discover if it is related to the matriarchal/patriarchal distinction. In each case

I have documented the categories I have chosen. Although I usually give only one source, there are in fact many sources and the extensive bibliography indicates others. The categories I give come from religious practices, but are described in their "ideal" rather than actual form: that is, there never has been a purely patriarchal religion, or a purely matriarchal religion. Religion is practiced by people, who bring to it their own experiences. Patriarchal religions had male and female followers and from earliest times had modified forms of the patriarchal ideal. I have drawn out the strictest implications of each category so that we can recognize it in any of its protean forms and understand its essential thrust, even in its softened presentation.

"Is God Male or Female?" is concerned with the status of these categories of opposition. Are they written into the very nature of things, inculcated by culture, or does the truth lie in between? If they are not innate, what options exist as ways of structuring reality? Three views are examined and rejected and then a new perspective is offered. This perspective, although it grew out of my experience with alternative views of reality, is really independent of the whole argument and should be viewed as a personal epilogue.

1
The Frankenstein Motif

RELIGION HAS a threefold concern:[1] cosmology—
how people came to be and how they fit into the scheme of
things; consolation—assurance that people's experiences
are meaningful and ultimately justifiable; and ethics—universal moral judgments and guidance, showing how people
ought to live. The first component, cosmology, is often considered pseudo-science and is indeed often treated pseudo-
scientifically. At best, the origin of human existence is
thought to be the object of mere curiosity. But people's
need to discover whether their existence is accidental or
planned and whether they are loved or rejected is more
than curiosity. This is true on the cosmic level as much as
it is on the personal level.

The subject of cosmology is crucial to our understanding
of ourselves and it derives its importance through its inti-
mate connection with the other two components of religion,
consolation and ethics. It is through our view of the meaning of life and of moral obligation that we define and
ultimately understand ourselves. However, these views
themselves grow out of their cosmology. If our origin is
accidental, then we must look within ourselves for both
meaning and a moral way of life. Similarly, if we are the
product of an indifferent or dissatisfied creator, we cannot

seek outside ourselves for consolation. But if the creator is like a parent, or more specifically, like a mother, then the creator is not only the cause of our being but the source of our consolation and moral guidance.

To the cosmological questions "How did I come to be?" and "What is my relationship to the cause of my being?" several possible answers may be offered. One is that humanity is the result of an accident—the spontaneous surfacing of consciousness in an unconscious and indifferent universe. This choice is necessarily rejected in all religious systems because accident precludes meaning and meaning is the underlying assumption of religion. The particular meaning may vary from one religion to another or it may be unrevealed. In that case, the religion teaches that while the purpose of life cannot be known, it exists nevertheless and genesis by accident is still ruled out.

Another cosmology with an accidental component is the emanationist theory. This view holds that the creator is so overflowing with being and goodness that he overflows into other creations, much as a fountain overflows into the layer beneath.[2] The emanationist view assures people of the fullness and goodness of their source and allows that human nature is formed directly of the nature of God. The drawback of the emanationist position is the unconscious nature of creation it presents. God, without deliberation, without even awareness of what he is doing, gives rise to offspring to whom he feels no responsibility for nurturance, protection, or guidance. While it may be possible to derive a moral code from an emanationist view, one cannot derive meaning, because of the accidental nature of creation. Religions have therefore rejected the emanationist cosmology in favor of a conscious creation.

One such cosmology, typical of patriarchal religious systems, portrays the creator as artist, and mankind as his work of art. This view is illustrated in the Old Testament. God, like a potter, fashions man from clay, views the finished product critically, and declares that it is good. The creation, man, is wholly external to and removed from the creator, God. Moreover, the creator is capable of an objective, even harsh, evaluation of his creation.

The idea of God as father is really a manifestation of the concept of God as artist. In both cases, the role played by God is that of spiritual progenitor and external judge. This contrasts with the idea of God as mother, whose role is that of physical progenitor and source of succor, protection, and uncritical acceptance. Noah's flood and the destruction of Sodom and Gomorrah are incompatible with a mother God; they are the result of God the father judging that his creation had gone awry. This is, of course, one of the difficulties arising from the model of God as artist. The artist may destroy his work because it does not live up to his concept of what the work should be.

Another difficulty is that the artist does not console or morally guide a work of art. Lack of consolation is seen in the so-called aesthetic theory of evil. Evil is held to be shading in a painting allowing brilliant colors to shine forth by contrast. Here religion fails in one of its main purposes, consolation. An individual is not consoled by feeling that his role may be to portray the shading. Also, though an individual will never see the finished painting, it clearly

means more to God than the particular individuals in the
cosmic canvas. This point is very forcefully made when
Job asks God for the meaning of his suffering. God's answer out of the whirlwind includes the proud description
of his creation, "Behold now Behemoth which I made as
well as you,"[3] and the charge that Job has no special claims
on his creator. God's one concession to Job is to give him
a personal tour of the canvas, to which Job responds, "I
had heard of you by hearsay, but now my own eyes have
seen you"[4] and is reconciled. The only consolation for Job
and for later generations of Jobs might be their assurance
of God's joy and pride in his creation, were it not for much
evidence to the contrary in other books of the Old Testament; the destruction in the Flood, at Babel, at Sodom and
Gomorrah, in the wilderness, and finally the destruction of
Jerusalem itself.

If the artistic model does not console, neither does it
offer moral guidance. A religious ethical code is built *in
imitatio Dei*. But if God's decisions are made for aesthetic,
not ethical, principles and the finished work is not revealed
to people, there is no way for human beings to learn the
right way to live. Nevertheless the artistic model is the
dominant one in the Judaeo-Christian tradition.

A remaining cosmology, portraying God as divine
mother, is the cornerstone of matriarchal religions. The
idea that primal man is born of woman is easily accepted
because it is a logical extension of human experience. The
mother-God is felt to provide comfort, protection, and consolation, because that is what a maternal figure is understood to represent. Moral guidance in a matriarchal system

comes directly from the mother through her identification with the mother-God.

It is easy to accept and worship a loving mother who nurtures and protects, but the view of God as mother is not without difficulties. Along with an experience of the fruitful goodness of the earth comes an awareness of evil, pain, and suffering. A religious system must provide a meaningful explanation for the presence of evil by somehow relating evil to the central figure of worship. But if God is portrayed as a nurturing mother, then evil cannot be related to the central figure and must be explained in terms of some weakness in her or in terms of other gods.

As patriarchal religion superseded the earlier matriarchal structure, the offspring of the body gave way to the offspring of the mind, and God as artist (or father) prevailed over God as mother. The transfer was never complete, however, and the concept of mother-God continued to develop.[5] This development occurred alongside and in complete contradiction to God the artist.

Monster or Offspring?

It is clear that the relationship of creator to creation is of fundamental concern in religion: (1) How did creation come about, by procreation or reason? (2) What is the substance of creation: the substance of the creator, the substance of the womb, or lifeless clay? Finally (3) How does the creator feel about the creation: was it good or did he repent in his heart that he had made it? The last question gives rise to the motif of *Frankenstein* by Mary Shelley. It is the story of a scientist giving life to a creature who then rises up to destroy its creator. The author treats Dr. Franken-stein's culpability in creating a monster and then aban-doning it, so that the once-benevolent creature becomes depraved. On one level, man recognizes himself as Dr. Frankenstein and acknowledges his ambivalence toward those whom he brings to life. On another level, people see themselves akin to the pitiable monster, benevolent until abandoned by God at the expulsion from Eden. They see in God's action at the Flood, at the destruction of Sodom and Gomorrah, and in God's temptation to kill all the Children of Israel in the desert, a creator dissatisfied with his creation. In that light, people recognize in themselves the depravity of the monster.

Humanity's view of itself, either little lower than the angels or innately evil, is directly related to its view of God's judgment of creation. The crucial question becomes "monster or offspring?" It is within this framework that the modes of creation in matriarchy (God as mother) and patri-archy (God as artist) must be compared.

The problem of the relationship of creator to creature must also be examined from a different aspect. One of the most important but frustratingly ambiguous statements in the Bible is that man is made in the image of God: ". . . in the divine image created he him, male and female created he them."[6] In what sense are humans God-like? Most often the human aspect judged to be God-like is creativity. If God is the creator and humans are made in his image, then hu-man divinity is in creativity. But if humans stand toward their creations as God does toward his, then the question of

God's relationship to his creation is crucial because we learn how to relate to our creations *in imitatio Dei,* modeling our relationship on God's. The three central religious concerns then reappear in a new form: (1) What is God's creation, the perfect realm of ideas or this material world? Do humans accept as divine the creations of the mind or those of the body? Or, in other words, are humans as artists divine or are humans as parents divine? (2) Is God satisfied by his creation and does he allow it to grow to independence, or does he stand in awful judgment of it? Do humans instill independent life and will and allow their creatures to rise up before them, or do they, when they see "creation gone awry," destroy it? This particular problem arises repeatedly in the Bible in terms of actual and attempted cases of infanticide[7] (which parallel God's punitive judgments on his creatures[8]) and in the law of the rebellious son in Deuteronomy 21:18: "If a man has a stubborn and rebellious son . . . then all the men of the city shall stone him to death . . ." (3) Is creation an ongoing process and are humans partners in creation or must creatures remain creatures and the desire for partnership be indicative of hubris, pride, the sin of the fallen angels? Do humans create themselves and take responsibility for what they become or do they accept the station in life allotted to them, in an incomprehensible but foreordained plan?

So humanity, in the ambiguous role of creature and creator, attempting to live in imitation of God, faces the question of the relationship of creator to creature in an especially urgent fashion. In this context the almost archetypal theme of Frankenstein's monster becomes important to consider.

Frankenstein's monster is not the first being created by reason alone with

> The tender core from which life used to surge,
> The gracious force that came from inward urge,
> Which took and gave, for self-delineation,
> Blending near traits with far in new mutation.[9]

Goethe's homunculus and the Jewish *golem* are other instances of artificial humans.

The Golem

In considering the question of the imitation of God, the Jewish concept of the *golem* is the most instructive.[10] The *golem* is another homunculus or magic creature, a theme with enduring fascination. The only Biblical reference to the *golem* is a highly ambiguous reading in Psalm 139:16: *Golmi ra'u 'enekha* ("Your eyes beheld my life stages").[11] The Talmud, however, takes up the concept in a most insightful way. The *golem*, fashioned as it was not in the womb of a mother but in the lifeless earth, is flawed, imperfect, matter without form. Adam, the original being fashioned from clay, is called a *golem*, but along with his flawed nature comes a power of grasping or understanding bound up with the nature of the earth from which he is made. In other words, the flaw in the *golem* is not an intellectual flaw. It is a lack of spirit or soul. A creator of a *golem* can give it vitality but not soul.

Despite the Biblical mention of the *golem* and the Talmudic discussion, the real development of the concept is a product of a much later environment—medieval German Jewry. The *golem*, in medieval Jewish tradition, is created by the magical force of God's secret name (the word). Originally the creation of a *golem* was part of the mystic's ecstatic trance and formed part of his experience of the creation. The *golem* had no external objective existence. Later, however, the *golem* was seen to be an external creature, resulting from the magic spells of the mystic. With the externalizing of the *golem*, the unrestrained power of an animate but soulless creature was experienced. The mystics, fearful of what they had given rise to, sent it back to the dust from whence it came. There is a fearful irony here, for what was originally intended by the creation of the *golem* was a life *in imitatio Dei*. God created by the word and the mystics sought to do likewise. The frightening conclusion was that the creation went awry and the mystics restored it to lifeless dust. This act was again in imitation of God, but now the imitation was unconscious.

Imitation of God has always been the mystic goal, so the mystic's life depended upon his view of the divine life. For the followers of the Zohar (the major work in later Jewish mysticism), the divine life was the life within the family. Creation was viewed sexually and therefore human sexuality became a sacred act. Love, procreation, and instructing one's children were of the highest concern. These views contrast sharply with those of the medieval German Jewish mystics. They held that creation was achieved by the potency of the divine name, "the word," and this belief accounts for their preoccupation with making a *golem*. They were ascetics, whose practice specifically included the renunciation of playing with children. The children of the body were rejected in favor of spiritual children.

One serious implication of the choice of the mode of creation is the attitude toward the flesh. When creation is "out of the body," the body is seen as holy, and sex is (*in imitatio Dei*) a holy and sacred obligation. When creation is by "word" and "the word is made flesh," then the flesh is not part of the essence of the divine word; it contains and imprisons the divine word, but does not partake in divinity. The flesh is viewed as an impediment to perfection as in the expression "the spirit is willing but the flesh is weak." It is seen as the source of all human weakness, or even as the demonic in man. This is part of the Frankenstein motif. Because Frankenstein creates the monster by use of reason, he cannot relate to the monster's deformed flesh. When he speaks with the monster, averting his eyes, he recognizes the justice of the monster's cause. But, "When I looked upon him, when I saw the filthy mass that moved and talked, my heart sickened and my feelings were altered to those of horror and hatred."[12]

What can be learned from the stories of Frankenstein and the *golem*? Three questions of cosmological concern can be partially answered: (1) How did creation come about? It is now clear that the answer "by word alone" is fraught with danger. Word alone can create a monster as well as a human. (2) What is the substance of creation? For a *golem*, it is lifeless substance, but for a human, it must be the substance of life. (3) How does the creator feel about the creation? If the creation is external, following the artistic model, then the creator judges his artistic effort and may destroy it. When the creator creates humans in this external way, they will necessarily be less in God's image than if they had been created from God as parent, that is from the very substance that makes God. In fact, the creation may be totally other than the creator, thus giving rise to the alienated view, "God's ways are not our ways." Related to this is the possibility that the creation may be flawed. When the creation is strictly physical, something of the creator goes into the creation and the creator recognizes a little of himself in his creation. However when the creation is external, then the creator is judgmental and may be estranged from it or see it as other than himself. He may not feel any obligation to nurture or teach it, but believe that merely creating it is sufficient to earn his creature's gratitude. Thus, when Dr. Frankenstein's mother gave birth to *him*, she and her husband felt a "deep consciousness of what they owed towards the being to which they had given life," but when Frankenstein considers creating monsters he is certain that "no father could claim the gratitude of his child so completely as I should deserve theirs."[13] His concern is with their gratitude toward him, not his obligation to them. Finally, when the creation is flawed because the creator has not fully given of himself, he comes to abhor it and wishes that he had never created it and may even destroy it.

The Two Adams

In the Judaeo-Christian scriptures there are two significant instances of unnatural birth—the creation of Adam and the incarnation of Jesus, who is also referred to as the second Adam. There are actually two differing accounts of creation in Genesis. In the first account, creation is by word. This account is the logical culmination of the earlier Babylonian tradition. In the Babylonian epic Enumah Elish, there is a female god, Tiamat, whose presence suggests an earlier matriarchal tradition. She is killed by her grandson, Marduk, who then creates the world out of her body. At this stage of the story the substance of creation is still one with the gods. Later in the story, however, Marduk must submit to the test of creating and then destroying a garment *by word alone.* Since he had already killed the supreme goddess and had already created the world, this would seem to be a superfluous test for proving his supremacy. What it does represent is the decisive move from God as parent to God as artist. The supreme god no longer creates from the body but must prove that he can create from the spirit or "by word alone." In the opening words of Genesis the conflict has been resolved—"God *said* 'let there be light' " and all the rest of creation is accomplished in the same manner.

This account, however, does not allow for a special relationship between man and God—man and the cattle were created in the same way. This "deficiency" is rectified in the second account of creation in Genesis 2:4–7. There God fashions Adam out of clay and "breathes life" into him. This concept of breath is related to *psyche*, the Greek concept of soul. Until Adam is "besouled" by the breath of God, he will not be fully alive or fully human. While the process of breathing life into Adam overcomes the *golem* aspect to an extent, the question remains whether it is a sufficient personal donation from the creator. Is this creation sufficiently different from that of the animals and trees that man can establish a special relationship with God? Based on the evidence of the Old Testament, the conclusion is that it is not. Even in this second account of creation, creation is not of the body. This admits the possibility that the creator may judge the creation to be flawed, a concept specifically recognized in Genesis. After the flood, when God pledges never again to destroy all of his creation, his justification is that man is flawed from the start and cannot be held responsible for his defective nature. God thereby takes responsibility for the flaw in creation.[14] The other supernatural creation of human life in the Judaeo-Christian scriptures is the birth of Jesus in the New Testament. While the first Adam is created externally by God, the second Adam, Jesus, is formed in the maternal womb, a return to matriarchal material creation, allowing the possibility for creation of the perfect human.

The issue of returning from the patriarchal model of God as artist to the matriarchal model of God as parent is charged with emotion. Not unexpectedly, many of the earliest heresies concerned the nativity of Jesus.[15] One heresy attempts to transform the story of the conception and birth of Jesus into a philosophical doctrine in which *sophia*, or pre-existent knowledge, is actualized in the flesh of Jesus. Those that focused on the "flesh" were equally concerned lest the story of the birth of Jesus be compared to the stories of the births of pagan heroes who claimed one of the gods as a father. They tried to show in what way God, as father of Jesus, differed from Zeus, as father of Aiakos.

As we have seen, patriarchal creation "by word" leads to the serious problems of estrangement and flawed creation without moral responsibility by the creator. The doctrine surrounding the nativity of Jesus can be viewed as a step toward feminization of the Old Testament patriarchy. It is a doctrine beset with logical and philosophical difficulties, not the least of which is the role of Mary (to be discussed further). Yet as a model of the relationship of God to man, it survives the theoretical problems.

Christians were not alone in feeling a need for "softening" the harsh patriarchal cosmology. The Zohar (see chapter 5) rejects creation by word alone in favor of a sexual model. This served to sanctify human sexuality and family life for the Jewish mystics and answered their needs of consolation and guidance. Christian medieval mystics were greatly preoccupied with the question of *creatio ex nihilo*, creation out of nothing. John Scotus Erigena holds that "creation out of nothing" means creation out of God, because God is the Great Nothing—that which cannot be defined (no thing).[16] Erigena has transformed the patriarchal, nonphysical concept of creation out of nothing into the concept of creation out of God. Christian doctrine dictates that Christ is of the same substance as God; Erigena is arguing that this is true for all mankind. The implication for Jesus of being one substance with God is that he can be perfect; the implication for mankind would be the same. Thus Erigena's position that creation is out of the very substance of the creator represents a return to the concerned matriarchal view of creation.

The spectrum of humanity's view of itself ranges from monster to diety. The key to its self-image lies in its source.

2
The Eleusinian Mysteries

WE HAVE LOOKED at views of creation and their
implications for concepts of self and relationship to the
world as a whole. The two major views exemplified in religion are matriarchal and patriarchal. The matriarchal view
flourished in Greece in the form of the Eleusinian Mysteries.

The Cult of Eleusis was one of the major religions in
Greece for a period of almost two thousand years. Tradition
places the introduction of this cult of Demeter to the second half of the fifteenth century B.C. It grew and flourished,
making Eleusis, home of the sanctuary, a major religious
center in the pagan world. The Homeric Hymn to Demeter,
now believed to be the official story of the religion, was re-
corded in the seventh century B.C. The religion reached its
peak in the Roman Imperium.[1]

When Christianity came to Greece, the Eleusinian Mysteries began to decline. In the fourth century A.D. strict laws
were enacted against secret cults—this must have hurt the
secret temple worship. In the fifth century A.D. Christians
built a church in the sacred temple area of Eleusis,
scratched crosses in the marble of the ruined temple, and
buried their dead in the once sacred area.[2] A religion which
had served humanity and which humanity served for two
thousand years had died. Moreover, it apparently disap-

peared without any record of what the religion was about. The hymn remains, its interpretation lost; the Mysteries have remained a mystery.

However, it should be possible to reconstruct the elements of the religion, both through knowledge of our own needs and by traces in the religion that supplanted it. To reconstruct the Eleusinian Mysteries may be a valid enterprise in its own right, although surely it would be a task more appropriate for a classicist than a philosopher. My interest in the Mysteries is that in a major respect it differs from the dominant religion in Western culture. The Cult of Eleusis is a matriarchal religion and its central figures are female. The Judaeo-Christian religion is patriarchal; its major figures are male. How significant is this difference? What does it imply for religion as a whole? The Eleusinian Mysteries met a need, which is why the cult lasted as long as it did. Nevertheless, it was supplanted by Christianity. What did Christianity mean to an initiate of the Mysteries? What need did the Mystery Cult of Eleusis cease or fail to meet that made the initiates willing to convert? Extrapolating from the Eleusinian Mysteries, what conclusions can we draw about matriarchy and patriarchy in contemporary religion?

The Hymn to Demeter

The major story in the Eleusinian Mysteries is the story of Demeter and Persephone. Persephone, the daughter of the goddess Demeter, is abducted by Pluto, the god of Hades.

Persephone shrieks out as she is carried away, and Demeter
hears her cry and begins to search for her daughter. For
nine days she searches, unable to locate her. Finally Helios,
the sun god, whose beams go everywhere, tells Demeter
that Pluto has abducted Persephone. He tells Demeter
not to mourn, because Pluto is not really an unfit husband
for Persephone, that he is Demeter's own brother, and is
extremely important. But Demeter, inconsolable, wanders
the earth in mourning.

   The next part of the story brings Demeter to the town of
Eleusis. Demeter comes to rest in Eleusis, is comforted, in-
structs the people to build a temple for her (for she will not
return to Olympus), and teaches them the rites of her awesome mysteries. Now that Demeter has a place to dwell, her
temple at Eleusis, she seeks to punish Zeus and the other
Olympian gods for the loss of her daughter. Humans become the instrument of her revenge for, as Demeter knows,
the gods need sacrificial offerings. She causes a "dreadful
and cruel year" in which the soil will not bear anything,
thereby robbing the gods on Mount Olympus of the rites
of sacrifice. She refuses to let fruit spring out of the ground
until she can once again behold Persephone. Hermes, in the
role of intercessor, goes down to Hades and persuades Pluto
to release Persephone. Pluto, however, gives Persephone a
pomegranate seed which she unwittingly eats. Because she
has eaten in the underworld, she must spend one season, or
a third part of the year, with Pluto in Hades. The other two
parts of the year she will spend with Demeter. Demeter
once again allows the land to be fruitful. One third of the

year it is not fruitful, the third that Persephone is under-
ground; but two thirds of the year it brings forth fruit.

What does this story mean to the initiates? On a simple
level, one can understand the story of Demeter as an agricultural fertility myth, that is, each year the land brings
forth, but each year it appears to die. How can we be assured of its continued renewal? How can we rejuvenate the
land? This hardly seems an adequate understanding of a
religion dominant in a civilization that produced the most
profound philosophers and playwrights of Western culture,
all of whom lived in cities, far removed from the land. We
know too much about the language of symbol to rob a
religion of its transcendent aspect. The Cult of Demeter at
Eleusis was developed over a period of two thousand years
in a literate cosmopolitan culture. If it could appeal to the
major intellectuals of the time (and we know that Plato, for
example, was an initiate of the Mysteries), its fundamental
story was more than an agricultural myth.

The interpretations we find by symbolists (Freud and
neo-Freudians) and the special class of symbolists, structuralists (Claude Lévi-Strauss), are fascinating. The structuralists in particular give us profound insights into the
relationships between seemingly unrelated myths; for example, Oedipus and the Garden of Eden. These insights are
provocative and instructive but, again, they operate on a
different level from the way the story "works" for the be-
liever. The structuralist's explanation is made in terms of
pointing out categories of opposition (Demeter and Pluto;
stasis and change) and showing the underlying conflict

handled by these categories. This approach has a great deal
to support it. For believers, however, these factors are not
conscious elements in their belief and may not even be
present at all. It is as if one deeply moved by a Bach organ
work were told that he or she was moved because the theme
developed into a fugue, modulated, and was recapitulated
in the minor. Undoubtedly Bach needed these techniques,
but the techniques are not what the work "meant" to the
listener, and in the final analysis do not explain why he or
she was moved.

Overcoming Death

Whether or not we use the formal analytic tools of the
structuralists, they as well as Freud do give us a significant
clue to what the Demeter text, as well as all religious texts,
are about. Freud has told us that the major conflict is between *eros* and *thanatos*: loving, reproducing, joining ever
larger groups—or escaping into death.[3] Lévi-Strauss also
points out the same basic concern with death. The function
of every central story of a culture, he suggests, is to reconcile its adherents to the existing situation. Specifically, if we
were to die much sooner, that would create disorder and
meaninglessness; were we to die much later, that would
create a different sort of chaos. We are to be convinced that
the time we have is not too long, not too short, but "just
right."[4] Or, as another symbolist, Leach, puts it, religion is
preoccupied with the paradox that life leads to death. It
seeks to deny that life necessarily turns into its opposite,
death, by creating a third alternative. This alternative is the

mystical idea of "another world," a land of the dead where
life is perpetual.[5] Whether religion's solution is, as Leach
says, "another world," the problem is the same: How can
man be reconciled to death?

I suggest there are three ways we deal with death:

(1) Death is not inevitable, but is in fact attractive and
we voluntarily choose it. This surprising approach is convincingly discussed by Freud in "The Theme of the Three
Caskets," where he sees it not only in religion, but as an
underlying motif in the stories collected by the Brothers
Grimm.[6]

(2) Another way is to accept personal death for the sake
of immortality through one's offspring. In effect, the story
of the Garden of Eden is the story of death as a necessary
result of sexual knowledge. Prior to eating of the fruit of
the Tree of Knowledge, Adam and Eve were unaware of
their nakedness and so couldn't bear children. This is made
clearer when God tells Eve that as a direct result of her
eating of the fruit, she will bear children (sometimes interpreted as a punishment, but should be seen as an objective
account of the responsibility resulting from her new awareness). This relationship of death to childbearing, implicit in
Genesis, is explicit in the African cosmology story "The
Stone, the Turtle, and the Man." God asks the stone if it
chooses to have children. The stone chooses immortality.
God next asks the turtle, who chooses to have children.
Man, shamed by the turtle's selfless choice, chooses also to
have children, and that is why he is not immortal.

(3) Finally, one can deal with death by denying its abso-
luteness. It is reversible; it can be overcome. It is to remove

the terrible antinomy—that to be alive is to be moving
toward death—that many of the stories in religion are formulated.

So the three apparent choices are to choose death because
in some way it really is the fairest of them all; to accept
death and be reconciled by having children; and to see
death not as irreversible, but as something that can be overcome. On this basis, we can now understand the story of
the Cult of Demeter in terms of how people are reconciled
to their own death, and it is in this sense that the story has
a very powerful motif. Demeter searches so hard for Persephone and tries to rescue her from the underworld not
because Persephone is pure and good, but because Persephone is her daughter. In other words, god is Persephone's
mother. If god is a mother, then by trying to keep Persephone from dying she isn't rewarding her, she is doing
what she must do. Her desperate attempts at salvation
spring from her motherly concern and not from her judgment that Persephone is worthy or had followed certain
commandments. Demeter becomes a symbol of what we all
want: to have someone fighting for our eventual triumph
over death. It is important to note that the Demeter story
does not deny death or its awfulness. Death is real and
powerful and Demeter cannot keep Persephone from dying.
She can only keep Death's triumph from being final. Persephone dies, but having been buried, rises again.

As mentioned before, a number of scholars have claimed
that the story of Demeter and Persephone is basically an
agricultural myth, based on an old fertility rite. It is true
that the rites of the Eleusinian Mysteries can be understood

as fertility rites, and, in fact, probably did originate as just that. It is also true that Christ is buried and rises again just as the vernal equinox, which heralds the planting season, comes around. While there was a relationship between agriculture and the Christian Passion, this is no longer the meaning attached to the rite, but rather it serves as a powerful symbol for something else. This interpretation is as true in understanding the Eleusinian Mysteries as it is in Christianity. This "something else" is our way of dealing with death.

The Traces of Eleusis

To further understand the Mysteries, we look for its traces in the religion that supplanted it. In the Greek Orthodox ritual there is a practice unique to Greek Christian observance, and probably has Greek rather than Christian origin. On Easter Sunday morning, a priest ignites many torches while speaking the words "He is risen." In all reports of the Eleusinian Mysteries, we read of a torchlight search for Persephone. Demeter goes in search of her daughter and joyfully proclaims "She is risen."[7] There are more important traces to be found. To do so, we must confront the differences between patriarchy and matriarchy. We must also try to discover how the initiates of the Cult of Demeter understood Christianity.

In matriarchy, the most important relationship is between mother and child—a relationship that carries with it an absolute obligation. The worst crime is infanticide; the second worst, matricide. In other words, you have an abso-

lute obligation to those in your blood line. In patriarchy, the
concern is not for the blood line; rather it is for absolute
ethical principles. In matriarchy, God is a mother frantically
trying to save her child. In patriarchy, God is a father who
is both creator and destroyer. He is the one who saves you,
but he can also condemn you. Salvation depends on an
ethical judgment. Salvation in patriarchy also depends upon
being "made in my image." The concept "made in my image" is essential to partriarchy because while a woman can
never doubt that she is the mother, a man can never be sure
of his paternity, and the only convincing evidence is the
physical resemblance of offspring. So, "made in my image"
was originally meant in a literal sense. By extended usage,
however, "made in my image" came to mean "shares my
values," and it became an ethical judgmental term. A woman
accepts her child unjudgmentally. Traditionally, it has been
assumed that a man is very ambivalent about his child. He
sees his child as a rival and a threat. This is one of the
major conflicts worked out in the Bible, where there are
repeated incidents of attempted and actual infanticide, and
attempts to mitigate it with some genuine sense of the importance of the role of the father. In any event, what has
emerged from the conflict between matriarchy and patriarchy has been an emphasis on the distinction between the
unconditional and the judgmental positions. In matriarchy,
one is saved because of a relationship; in patriarchy, one is
saved because of an ethical judgment.

Another major difference between the matriarchal Eleusinian Mysteries and the patriarchal Christian religion is in
their view of death. Christianity focuses on the cross—the

cross is what kills; the Eleusinian Mysteries on the seed—
the seed brings forth life.[8] This is a crucial difference if
religion's major concern is to reconcile us to our death. If
we analyze the actual structure of the stories and the roles
of their central characters, significant differences appear.
The Eleusinian drama is basically the drama of life and
death. Life is "played" by Demeter, and once again by the
land's renewed fertility. Death is represented both by Pluto,
the god of Hades, and by the land cursed to barrenness by
Demeter. Between these two opposing positions are two
intercessors or mediators: Persephone, who alternates between life and death, and the seed, which must be buried
but which brings forth life. At first glance, the story seems
to have the same structure as the Christian Passion, but if
we analyze it, some important differences can be found.
Using the same approach with the Passion story, we find
very different categories of opposition. The roots of the opposition lie in the Old Testament, when the continuum
from God to man is destroyed. Prior to the Flood, there had
been three kinds of beings: sons of God, daughters of men,
and an intermediary sort of being who was the offspring of
the union of the two. This little-recognized point is unambiguously stated in Genesis 6:1–4. All of these "intermediary" beings were destroyed in the Flood. As a result, an
opposition between God and man, creator and creature,
perfect and imperfect, is created. So God (who is in an
analogous position to Demeter) has as his opposite not
death, but man. Christ as intercessor is not the intercessor
between God and death, but between God and man.

The analogy breaks down in yet another crucial way.

Christianity, faced with the paradox of life leading to death, creates the third alternative of "another world." The attributes of this "other world" are necessarily not of this world: this is a world of time, Heaven is timeless; this is a world of change, Heaven is changeless; since this is a fertile world, then Heaven must be barren and infertile. So Heaven is defined not in opposition to Hades, but in opposition to life, and in most important ways is identical to Hades. When Persephone dies and rises, her triumph is over Hades. When Christ dies and rises, his triumph is over life.

Thus the emphasis in the Eleusinian Mysteries is on this life and this world. The view in Christianity is that the real life is not in this world, but is in the world to come. In terms of the three choices for dealing with death, we find the first in Christianity and the remaining two in the Cult of Demeter. The Eleusinian Mysteries, by making central the relationship of parent to child, emphasizes the possibility of living on through one's children. It also holds that death can be overcome, that one rises again. The Christian view is that death is not really death and so we willingly choose it: that this is a pilgrim world through which we are only passing:

> The Christian optimism is based on the fact that we do *not* fit into the world. . . . The modern philosopher had told me again and again that I was in the right place, and I had still felt depressed even in acquiescence. But I had heard that I was in the *wrong* place, and my soul sang for joy, like a bird in spring. . . . I knew now why grass had always seemed to me as queer as the green beard of a giant, and why I could feel homesick at home.[9]

Christianity's rejection of this material world in favor of another world leads to a rejection of the physical creation of human beings. Christianity does not envy woman's creation, which is analogous to the motherhood of nature, but chooses celibacy and sees it as the desired state.

So in two major respects the Eleusinian Mysteries and Christianity differ: first, salvation open to everyone simply by a relationship to God versus salvation based upon an ethical judgment; and second, the focus on this life, this world, and its material aspects versus focus on a world to come.

Christianity Through the Eyes of Eleusinians

Given these differences, what did Christianity mean to an initiate of the Cult of Demeter? How is it that Christianity could supersede the earlier religion? One very interesting point is that none of the converts to Christianity revealed the Mysteries. We know this because we have writings by the early Church Fathers speculating about what the Mysteries were and giving opposing hypotheses. Why didn't converts reveal the Mysteries? My hypothesis is that they did not see Christianity as being in conflict with the Mysteries. They saw Christianity as a reformulation of the Mysteries, and so were able to retain both religions. The major factor that had led to mystery religions in the first place was a concern with death and a need for salvation and Christianity shared this concern. But we have shown that the Cult of Demeter was matriarchal, and its concept of salvation different from that of patriarchal Christianity. But is Christianity really patriarchal, or can it be understood in some way to be matriarchal? Here we must choose an unorthodox interpretation, though one that has reappeared throughout the history of Christianity. Christ could, under some circumstances, be understood to represent the feminine aspect of God. In one sense, the strict patriarchy of the Old Testament is tempered somewhat in the New Testament. Adam is created by word alone (with the classical patriarchal rejection of body), but Christ, the second Adam, is begotten of woman. Nevertheless, this is not sufficient to allow for a matriarchal interpretation.

We have seen that one of the major aspects of a matriarchal religion is salvation based on being a child of God and not on merit. There are two passages in the New Testament that deal with essentially the same point: the parable of the vineyard laborers and the three parables of God's mercy found in the Gospel according to Luke: the lost sheep, the lost drachma, and the prodigal son.[10] In the parable of the vineyard laborers, a farmer hires men to work in his vineyard. After the third hour, he hires additional men; after the sixth and ninth hours he again hires more; and finally, at the eleventh hour, he hires still more men. At the twelfth hour, he pays each man a full day's wages. The emphasis in the parable is on the farmer's gratuitous generosity (God's gratuitous grace). Those who came in at the eleventh hour did not merit full payment but are rewarded, not because of merit, but because of God's love. Luke, the Gospel which emphasizes Christ's loving-kindness, gives three parables of God's mercy. The parable of the prodigal son is the most familiar and shows the matriarchal feeling most clearly. The son squanders his inheritance and leads a life of debauchery. When the money is gone and he feels pangs of hunger, he returns repentant to his father. Before he can even deliver his rehearsed speech of contrition, the father interrupts and in words closely analogous to Demeter's says, "My son was dead, and is alive again; he was lost and is found." They begin to celebrate. In contrast to the prodigal, his dutiful brother stands apart, unable to understand the rejoicing. His father simply repeats, "Your brother was dead and is alive; he was lost and is found."

In short, the Greeks found within Christianity the same assurance of salvation that they had found in their own mystery religion. Their matriarchal interpretation of Christianity reappears in the Reformation. In a sense, the whole Reformation can be understood in the light of the essential conflict between good works (which is patriarchal) and faith alone (which is matriarchal). Luther insisted that not by good works but by faith alone shall you be saved.

Why Christianity Triumphed

The question remains, what did Christianity hold for the Greeks that the Eleusinian Mysteries did not? We have said that dealing with death was the central concern of both religions, but what specifically is man's problem with death? As mentioned earlier, Lévi-Strauss writes that the purpose of myth is to convince us that the time between birth and death is just right. Just right for what? Just right to create meaning; for our real concern is that this all "be for something." This is why twentieth-century existentialists, such as Camus and Heidegger, are so preoccupied with death, asserting that it robs life of all meaning. They did not newly discover death or find it more pervasive than it had been in earlier times. People in the past could be reconciled to death if they saw a meaning or purpose to it. But if there is no value and people alone create meaning and value, then that meaning dies when they die; they cannot be part of something larger than their own life and effort. The existentialist denial of objective value is precisely what the Greeks experienced, for they felt that if everyone is saved, then there is no real difference between the good person and the evil person. To say that there is no difference between good and evil is to fly in the face of directly felt experience. As E. R. Dodds points out, there was an overwhelming sense of guilt and need for atonement in pagan Greece.[11]

It is hard to know why a culture develops a sense of guilt. It may grow out of an unbearable conflict between the culture's professed values and its actions. This was the case when the great democracy of Athens slaughtered the adult males of the neutral island of Melos and put the women and children into slavery. It may grow out of a breakdown in community and a need for personal values that transcend local norms. Whatever the reason, the Greeks developed a need for repentance. It was not enough for them to know that they were children of God, even if it meant salvation. They also had to know whether a person could repent. It is this question that the Eleusinian Mysteries could not answer, because the religion had no sense of atonement. Christianity, as a consequence of its patriarchal nature, has

a sense of sin and therefore a concept of atonement. Para-
doxically, the judgment we fear is also the judgment we
seek. There are times that persons judge their own behavior
and find themselves worthy or unworthy. Demeter makes
no such distinction, but Christianity does. It is the judgment of the Christian God which, while presenting the
difficulty of condemnation, was nevertheless necessary for
the Greeks at that time. The Greeks had a desire for a moral
code with theological sanctions, a desire for atonement, and
an awareness of the necessity of judgment, but with the
mitigating assurance that the prodigal son will be joyfully
welcomed back.

What does this teach us about the concepts of matriarchy
and patriarchy in contemporary religion? It tells us that
patriarchal religions without a sense of the personal concern
of parenthood are too harsh and that matriarchal religions
with their unqualified love are not morally satisfying.
Clearly some sort of mediation is needed: patriarchal religions need a feminine component, and matriarchal faiths
need a more abstract standard.

A more difficult task is to reconcile the two opposing
views of death. One says value lies in this world and this
life, while the other chooses dying to this world for the sake
of another. Yet, I suggest that a mediation can be found.
This world can be found valuable, this life good, but its
value and goodness are not exhausted by its material reality.
This world is good not only for what it is, but for what it
points to: a concept of perfection, value, and design which
transcends our own particular experience but infuses it
with value.

3

The Sacrifice of Isaac

AS WE HAVE just seen, the story of Demeter and Persephone is central for explaining the relationship of people to God in the matriarchal Cult of Eleusis. The story of the sacrifice of Isaac plays the same crucial role in the patriarchal Judaeo-Christian tradition.

> God put Abraham to the test. He said to him, "Abraham!" "Ready," he answered. And he said, "Take your son, your beloved one, Isaac whom you hold so dear, and go to the land of Moriah, where you shall offer him up as a burnt offering on one of the heights that I will point out to you." . . . They came to the place that God had spoken of to him. Abraham built an altar there. He laid out the wood. He tied up his son Isaac. He laid him on the altar on top of the wood. He put out his hand and picked up the cleaver to slay his son. But an angel of Yahweh called to him from heaven, "Abraham! Abraham!" . . . "Lay not your hand upon the boy, nor do the least thing to him!" . . . As Abraham looked up, his eye fell upon a ram snagged in the thicket by its horns. Abraham went and took the ram and offered it up as a burnt offering in place of his son.[1]

It is generally agreed that the story of the binding of Isaac, as the attempted sacrifice is called in Genesis, is the

pivotal story for the founding of the Judaeo-Christian tradition. It is through this act that God consciously enters
history, chooses a people with whom to make his covenant,
and sets in motion the events that comprise this religious
tradition. The sacrifice story serves not only as the starting
point, but as a constant point of reference in the Old and
New Testaments. The story is invoked when God's mercy
is sought.[2] It is also viewed as prefiguring the crucifixion,
where the lamb of God is not the beast caught in the
thicket, but his only-begotten son. In this connection, it is
most interesting that an earlier Midrashic version of the
story of Isaac has been discovered in which Abraham's
hand is not stayed, Isaac dies, is buried, and rises again on
the third day.[3]

While it is agreed that the story is pivotal, there is less
agreement as to what it means, other than representing a
"test" for Abraham. The degree of confusion and discom-
fort the story aroused in Talmudic times can be gauged by
the legends that sprang up to "correct" and "supplement"
the original text.[4] One group of legends concerns the motivation for the testing of Abraham. After all, Abraham had
been tested when he had been asked to leave his native land
to follow an unknown God. Why this new test? The legend
"answering" this question is modeled on the prologue to
the Book of Job. Satan confronts God about his servant
Abraham. "And the Lord said unto Satan, 'From whence
comest thou?' and Satan answered the Lord, and said, 'From
going to and fro on the earth, and walking up and down in
it.' " Satan accuses man of serving God for his own benefit.
"Hast Thou seen Abraham, the son of Terah, who at first

had no children, and he served Thee and erected altars to Thee . . . And now his son Isaac is born to him, he has forsaken Thee." God responds, as he does concerning Job, "Hast thou considered my servant Abraham? For there is none like him in the earth, a perfect and an upright man before me . . . As I live were I to say unto him, 'Bring up Isaac thy son before me,' he would not withhold him from me . . ." and the test is agreed upon.[5] What is particularly forceful about this legend is the conscious recognition that the testing of Abraham is so much like the testing of Job[6] This recognition of a shared theme led the legend makers to apply the structure of the story of Job back onto the Isaac story. The parallels between Isaac and Job will be further elaborated below.

Another group of legends concerns Sarah and her reaction to the attempted sacrifice. Sarah, barren all those years, is curiously absent in the Genesis account of the sacrifice. Sarah's barrenness was a source of great grief for her. She finally told Abraham, "Yahweh has restrained me from bearing. Cohabit then with my maid. Maybe I shall reproduce through her."[7] So Abraham cohabited with Sarah's maid, Hagar, and when Hagar saw that she was pregnant, she looked upon her mistress with contempt. Sarah at last conceived and bore Abraham a son in his old age and said, "Who would have said to Abraham that Sarah might nurse children! Yet I have borne a son in his old age."[8] And yet when Genesis takes up the narrative after Isaac is unbound, it is to give notice of the death of Sarah.[9] In a parallel situation in the Greek tradition, Clytemnestra slays her husband, Agamemnon, for sacrificing their daugh-

ter, Iphigenia.[10] Sarah's feelings are not alluded to in the
Bible, which focuses on Abraham's difficult trial, nor in
most commentaries, some of which consider Isaac's feelings.
Yet it was Sarah who had longed for a child and had re-
joiced when she bore a son in her old age. The legends
"correct" this omission in a curious way. In several versions, Satan informs Sarah that Abraham plans to sacrifice
Isaac. Upon hearing this news, Sarah almost dies of grief
but survives to await Abraham's return. When he returns
without Isaac, who has been taken directly to Paradise to
study God's ways, her worst fears are confirmed and she
dies of grief. In an interesting variation of this legend,
Sarah goes to Hebron to seek news of Isaac. When she
hears of his rescue, she expires out of pure joy. Whether
she dies of grief or joy, the legends are in agreement that
Sarah dies as a direct result of the binding of Isaac. Thus,
while the Bible implies a "happy ending" to the story, folk
tradition presents it as the direct cause of the death of
Sarah.[11] In doing so, the folk tradition points to an important truth: the sacrifice of Isaac did mean the death of
Sarah, in a sense that will be shown below.

Folk tradition supplies some background to the story of
Isaac and a look at the historical context supplies even
more. The sacrifice of offspring was not a unique event in
the cultures of the Near East and recurs also in Jewish history. Kings Ahaz and Manasseh both sacrificed their sons,[12]
and Jephthah his daughter.[13] Saul attempted to sacrifice his
son Jonathan, but was overruled by the people.[14] In Exodus
22:29–30, God clearly commands that "the first-born of
your sons you shall give to me. You shall do likewise with

your oxen and with your sheep." This commandment shows two things: first, just as first fruits of the soil are to be sacrificed to God, so are offspring; second, the relationship of father to son is one of proprietorship—the loss of a son is analogous to the loss of an ox or a sheep. This command, however, does not explain the sacrifice of Isaac, since he was not an infant at the time of the binding. But it does explain two other customs: the redemption of the first-born son and circumcision. The rite of circumcision could be understood as a substitute or token sacrifice of the son, the foreskin standing in the stead of the child. Infant sacrifices continued among the Jews in the times of the Temple and were railed against by the prophets Micah, Jeremiah, and Ezekiel.[15] It is likely that the sacrifices were surrogates for the king—the incarnate sun-god, who was to die each year. Death of the king, replaced by death of a surrogate king, and finally by animal sacrifice is well documented in the Greek tradition.[16]

Philosophers and theologians have dealt with the theme of the binding of Isaac in terms of the meaning of sacrifice and more specifically, the meaning of this unique sacrifice. We will examine several of these approaches in an effort to understand this most central of stories.

Relationship Through Sacrifice

Joseph Soloveitchik suggests an interesting interpretation of the meaning of sacrifice when he treats the creation of Eve out of Adam.[17] Why was Eve not created as Adam was (as, in fact, she was in the first creation account in Genesis)?

Why must Adam be put into the profound helplessness of sleep and lose a rib so that Eve might be created? Soloveitchik states that this mode of creation, entailing sacrifice, was to enable Adam to have a special relationship to Eve. More generally, he points out that it is through our self-sacrifices that committed and unique relationships are formed. Whether or not we accept Soloveitchik's interpretation of the creation of Eve, what insight does this concept of sacrifice add to the Isaac story? Although Abraham has several offspring, he has strong feelings only toward Isaac and, to a lesser extent, toward Ishmael. His other sons, Zimran, Jokshan, Medan, Midian, Ishbak, and Shuah, are not even mentioned at the time of his burial,[18] and as for any daughters Abraham may have had, they are not referred to at all. What do Isaac and Ishmael have in common that Abraham's other sons lack? The surprising answer is that both were nearly put to death by their father—Isaac, as we know, and Ishmael when Abraham sent him with his mother into the desert with only a loaf of bread and one skin of water. As in the Isaac story, an angel intervened and Ishmael was spared by the miraculous appearance of a well.[19] In matriarchy, a direct covenantal relationship between parent and child exists by reason of a blood tie. In Abraham's patriarchy, the father only becomes deeply related to his sons through a blood sacrifice—theirs.

In the Old Testament, sacrifice usually involves the one who offers it and the one who receives it. The thing being sacrificed, whether animate or inanimate, is regarded as an object. In the Abraham story, an important element is changed: the sacrificial object is a living human. Moreover, this sacrifice goes beyond the more widespread practice of infanticide. Isaac is of the age of sensibility and is able to walk unassisted, loaded down with wood, to the altar. This important change in the sacrifice concept results in a unique bond between Abraham and Isaac. Although Abraham had many sons, it was through the two with whom he had striven, whom he had attempted to kill and who nevertheless survived, that his inheritance is fulfilled. To go beyond struggle and to admit and accept parentage is the outcome of Isaac's redemptive sacrifice. The same type of redemptive sacrifice that Soloveitchik sees as necessary for a communal relationship between Adam and Eve can, in patriarchy, be applied as well to the concerned relationship of father to son.

A Knight of Faith

Kierkegaard deals with the sacrifice of Isaac by proposing a "teleological suspension of the ethical," that is, a temporary suspension of ethics for a special, higher purpose.[20] He argues that it is certainly unethical for Abraham to slay his son—the act countermands God's own commandment to Noah—but there is a value of faith of even higher value than "the good." Leaving aside the grave problems of subjectivity in Kierkegaard's approach, other difficulties remain. Abraham has apparently understood God's standards when he challenges him concerning the destruction of Sodom and Gomorrah: "Shall he who is Judge of all the world not act with justice?"[21] How can Abraham's challenge at Sodom and Gomorrah and subsequent silence at Mount Moriah be justifiable? At the time of the Sodom and Gomorrah challenge, God decides to make Abraham a part-

ner in his work and so to teach him his ways. "For I have
singled him out in order that he may instruct his sons and
his future family to keep the way of Yahweh by doing what
is just and right, so that Yahweh may achieve for Abraham
the promises he made about him."[22] Apparently Abraham
has understood God's ways, because when he challenges
God's decision to slay the righteous with the unrighteous,
God agrees with Abraham's reasoning and relents. So
Kierkegaard's concept of "knight of faith" does not suffice
to explain the Abraham who both challenges God and is
silent. In some manner both these actions must be justified
and the action of the silent Abraham needs further scrutiny. Assuming that Abraham is a "knight of faith" and
that this faith entails willingness to sacrifice Isaac, what is
it that Abraham has faith in? Implicit in Abraham's obedience is a belief in the value behind this obedience. God has
commanded him and he has obeyed ("Go forth from your
native land"); God has revealed his plan and he has challenged (Sodom and Gomorrah); God has commanded
("Sacrifice your son") and this command, coming after
Abraham's instruction in God's ways, must have been consistent with Abraham's understanding of God's ways. The
weakness in Kierkegaard's interpretation is that it regards
God's command to be paradoxical even though Abraham
himself did not.

Am I Abraham?

Sartre treats the question by reframing it for Abraham. Instead of asking himself, "Is this God who is demanding

that I sacrifice my son?" he asks, "Am I Abraham?" or, in other words, "Is this the role I should choose to act out? If I choose to sacrifice my son, then I create for myself a definition of myself as Abraham."[23] This is an important approach in that Sartre redirects the focus away from God and toward man. Imputing a command to God means that we believe it is something we must do—that it is right. Thus the importance of a command from God rests not in God or in the command, but in man's perception of the command. Sartre's view is that we define ourselves by what we do, that human beings have no essence, but create themselves by their actions. Merleau-Ponty expresses the same idea as, "You are what you do to others." But one needs to ask the further question, what does it mean to define oneself as Abraham? What is the essential element that makes one an Abraham? Sartre does not address that question and so fails to make sense of the central issue in the Abraham story.

Rabbi Menahem Mendl of Kotzk maintains that there was a twofold aspect to Abraham's test: the first was when he placed Isaac on the altar, the second, when he helped him down from it. The second trial, the releasing of Isaac, exacted greater strength than the first. "It took great self-control to miss such a marvelous opportunity to make a supreme sacrifice, and to yield to the angel."[24] Abraham's greatness consisted not only in his readiness to sacrifice Isaac at the call of the Lord, for anyone might have been aroused to ecstasy and done God's bidding. "But Abraham's exaltation had not subsided even on the third day after God's command. He had had time to reflect by then."[25]

Two things are very disturbing about this account: Why is it the greater trial to spare your son? and Why, three days after the command, is Abraham just as willing to go along with the sacrifice as he had been at the time of the initial order?

Beyond the Ego Boundary

David Bakan sheds some light on this question in his analysis of the sacrifice of Isaac. Bakan sees in the Old Testament an attempt to come to grips with the problem of the male's biological role in conception. The relationship of father to son exemplified by the father God to his children, Israel, is the continuing theme of the Old Testament. The hero is portrayed in his role as parent: Abraham, Isaac (whose character is only drawn out in his relationship to his sons, Esau and Jacob), and Jacob as the father of twelve sons. The Bible, in Bakan's terms, "expresses man's effort to extend the boundary of his ego to include his 'seed.' This particular metaphor for semen is interesting in that it not only suggests property and food, but also tends to make the male even more important than the female, as seed is the determining factor of the nature of the plant, with the soil, water, and sun playing only enabling roles."[26] Bakan's insight into the use of the metaphor "seed" brings to mind the argument in the trial of Orestes in Greek mythology which claims that "the parent is he who mounts." This is one of several parallels between the story of Abraham and the Oresteian Trilogy which opens with the story of the sacrifice of Iphigenia by her father, Agamemnon.

Two problems confront the patriarchs: How do they feel about their sons; do they acknowledge them as their own? and How do they deal with their own mortality? Can they extend their "ego boundaries" so that they live on through their seed, or do they "buy" immortality at the expense of their children?

Doubt over the authenticity of parenthood provokes the tendency to kill the child of doubtful parentage. Bakan suggests that there may have been some doubt as to the legitimacy of Isaac.[27] On two occasions, once before and once after the visit of the angels, Abraham conceals the fact that Sarah is his wife, allowing her to be married to someone else.[28] The possibility that Abraham might not have been the biological father of Isaac was even raised by Rabbi Solomon bar Isaac ("Rashi"), the distinguished eleventh-century Biblical commentator, although he refutes the idea.[29] Bakan points out that the same doubt may have prompted the apostle Paul to suggest, "Not all are children of Abraham because they are his descendents; but 'Through Isaac shall your descendents be named.' "[30] Finally there is a question surrounding the visit of the three angels.

Abraham hastened into the tent and called to Sarah, "Quick, three seahs of the best flour! Knead and make rolls!" With that, Abraham ran to the herd, picked out a tender and choice calf, and gave it to a boy, who lost no time in preparing it. Then he got some curds and milk, and the calf that had been prepared, and set these before them; and he stood by under the tree while they ate.

"Where is your wife Sarah?" they asked him. "In there, in the tent," he replied. Then one said, "When I come back to you when life would be due, your wife Sarah shall have a son!" Sarah had been listening at the tent entrance, which was just behind him. Now Abraham and Sarah were old, advanced in years; Sarah had stopped having a woman's periods. So Sarah laughed to herself, saying, "Withered as I am, am I still to know enjoyment—and my husband so old!" Yahweh said to Abraham, "Why did Sarah laugh, saying, 'Shall I really give birth, old as I am?' Is anything too much for Yahweh? I will be back with you when life is due, and Sarah shall have had a son!" Sarah dissembled, saying, "I didn't laugh," for she was afraid. But he answered, "Yes, you did."[31]

The words "which was just behind him" are usually regarded as referring to the door, but could refer instead to the angel, meaning that he was in the tent with Sarah.[32] Sarah's confused and shamed laughter, "for she was afraid," would make sense if what she feared was Abraham's suspicion that the child was not his. As it stands, her fear defies explanation. In any case, Abraham does accept Isaac as his son by applying to him the "mark of the covenant" in the form of circumcision. The ritual serves as a sign of possession and, by extension, a mark of legitimacy. Even so, Bakan suggests that doubt concerning Abraham's paternity of Isaac may have contributed to Abraham's motivation for sacrificing Isaac.

The question of immortality can be approached either through immortality of one's seed or through personal immortality. In the first case, one survives through one's children and one must therefore be directly concerned with their upbringing and care. Survival, then, is directly related to acceptance of one's adulthood and parenthood. The quest for personal immortality tends in the opposite direction. Survival is gained by being a child of the "Father in Heaven." Man defers to God so that God will not kill him as the child. "Taking the child's role spares one from the temptation of infanticide. Taking the child's role also opens up the possibility of endless life, since the termination of life has been converted into something dependent only on the sufferance of the 'father.' If he can be appeased, one might live forever. But taking the role of child means surrendering sexuality, reproduction, and one's own fatherhood—which, indeed, developed into an ideal of Christianity . . ."[33]

Talmudists recognized a relationship between the stories of Abraham and Job. The opening of the legendary version of the sacrifice of Isaac parallels the opening of Job: "Sovereign of the Universe, I have traversed the whole world and found none so faithful as thy servant Abraham."[34] Similarly, the Talmudic commentary on Job refers back to Abraham.[35] Bakan actually draws out some striking parallels in this implied relationship: Job and Abraham are presented principally as fathers; both have relationships to God in which the major concern is with offspring; three "men" visit Abraham and three comforters visit Job; both Abraham and Job are described as righteous; and both die at an advanced age.[36]

While both are "tested" by God, the nature of the test differs between the two. The test for Abraham is whether or not he would kill Isaac. The test for Job is how he would

respond to the killing of his children. Bakan suggests that
both stories are concerned with how men learn to deal with
their infanticidal impulses. If this is so, the answer is "not
very well," for it is not Isaac, the sacrificial lamb, who is
the moral exemplar, but Abraham; and Job finds new children fit substitute for those already slain, much as twelve
oxen represent adequate compensation for six slain ones.
The stories are not merely about Abraham and his son, or
Job and his. The central figure in both stories is God *as conceived by Abraham and Job*—God as the sanctioning force
behind the events. The story of the relationship of a father
to his son is "writ large," as it were, in the heavens. God,
the father, tests his offspring before he accepts them as
legitimate. The story must be regarded as a reflection of the
patriarchal view that the covenantal relationship is based
on sacrifice and not on blood ties.

Bakan's analysis of the sacrifice of Isaac is important. He
is clearly right that the relationship of father to son in the
Old Testament is a difficult one and that the "working out"
of this relationship is a central motif of the Bible. What is
less clear is that the Abraham story in any way explains or
points to a solution to this conflict. If a goal of the Old
Testament is to help fathers extend their ego boundaries to
include their sons, then the sacrifice of Isaac gives a contradictory message. The command to kill one's son and the
unquestioning compliance (which becomes paradigmatic for
devotion to God) cannot be instances of accepting one's son
and taking on the responsibility of fatherhood.

We must examine the sacrifice within its Biblical context
to try to determine what is actually at stake. The first com-

mand to Abraham is to go from his native land. Besides
showing that God has singled out a particular person for
his revelation, the command shows that Abraham has to
move away from an earlier tradition. God's revelation will
be in contradiction to the earlier tradition. One clue toward
an understanding of this earlier tradition lies in Abraham's
relationship to Sarah. "Sarah ranked higher than her husband."[37] According to the Jewish legends, Abraham owed
his flock and his herds as well as his position to his wife
Sarah.[38] Sarah is described as a Chaldean princess who
conferred status on Abraham by marrying him. Her death
"was a great loss to her country. So long as she was alive,
all went well in the land. After her death, confusion en-
sued."[39] If Sarah had been the mere consort of Abraham
her death would have had no tribal significance; but if the
legends really are the memory of an earlier tradition, this
tradition was matriarchy and the sacrifice of Isaac marked
the death of the matriarchal tradition personified by Sarah.

The meaning of Abraham's test becomes clear when
viewed in the light of the conflict between patriarchy and
matriarchy. The first allegiance in matriarchy is to one's
offspring, and by extension, to a blood relative. In patriarchy, the first obligation is to an abstract moral principle,
the voice of God. The meaning of the test is that Abraham
must prove his allegiance under the new, patriarchal system. Abraham, after all, had challenged God once on the
destruction of Sodom and Gomorrah (and saved his blood
relative, Lot). In order to prove that Abraham is not rooted
in the older tradition, God demands that he renounce the
most fundamental tenet of the matriarchal religion and kill

his own child. Abraham's choice is between the matriarchal
principle of protecting his child and the patriarchal principle of following an abstract ethic, obedience to God. Abraham passes the test and is pronounced fit to be the father of
a new, patriarchal religion. This interpretation explains
why Genesis passes over Sarah in silence. It explains that to
be a "knight of faith" is to have faith in the patriarchal,
testing God. It explains that to be Abraham is to be the
father of patriarchy (or the indirect murderer of Sarah).
And it explains that it is harder not to kill Isaac than to slay
him, because a new faith is being forged, forged in fervor
and not yet with moderation. The last vestiges of the earlier
tradition must be unremittingly destroyed.

4

Wandering

THE EARLIER tradition, matriarchy, sprang from the view of the relationship of mother to child, but eventually included a perspective on such seemingly disparate subjects as soil, settlement, and cities.

Women have traditionally been associated with the soil, and along with this association goes an entire value system and way of "being in the world." It came about for two reasons. Women were the first planters and the first harvesters, men were nomads and hunters. The conflict between these two lifestyles is brought out clearly in the Old Testament, which demands nomadism as a prerequisite to the spiritual life. The soil, which in matriarchy had been revered as "homeland," is regarded in the scriptures as a temptation leading one away from the spiritual life.

Woman's special relationship to the soil is also expressed in the analogy between woman as mother and earth as mother. Woman, like soil, is capable of transformation mysteries. A transformation mystery is that unique process by which a qualitative change comes about. It allows for genuine novelty, not mere increase and decrease: something that was one thing becomes radically "other." The earth transforms the "dead" seed into a living harvest. With equal mystery, the juice of its fruit transforms into an in-

toxicant. Finally, its grasses yield grain that is transformed
into bread, the Sacred Host. It is with the sense of wonder
attached to these transformations that wine and bread feature in so many religious rituals.

There are three transformation mysteries attributed to
women, all of them associated with the blood.[1] First, the
blood of menstruation transforms the girl into a woman.
This change is not a quantitative change—she is not
merely a bigger girl—but a qualitative change in that she is
transformed from child to adult in a clearly marked way.
Pregnancy is the second blood mystery. According to the
primitive view, the embryo is built up from the blood,
which, as the cessation of menstruation indicates, does not
flow outward during pregnancy.[2] The third transformation
is the changing of blood into milk. Erich Neumann suggests
that this transformation is the foundation for the primordial mysteries of food transformation. As a consequence of
woman's own transformation capacities, it was she who
became responsible for the transformation of food by cooking, baking, and fermenting.

Because the transformations are not understood, because
they are mysterious and yet all-important for human survival, the possibility that they may fail to occur is often
raised in early religious writings. For example, as seen
earlier, the Homeric Hymn to Demeter describes barley
sown into the ground that does not rise up as a new crop,
but rots in the untransforming soil. Demeter restores—
transforms—the land to fruitfulness. The Old Testament
focuses on the barrenness of women whose miraculous
power of transformation is blocked by an angry god. This

occurs when God "close[s] fast every womb in the household of Abimelech on account of Sarah."[3] It occurs again in
the case of Sarah's own barrenness, in Rebecca's, Rachel's,
and Hannah's. In each case the barrenness is a sign from
God, overcome only through God's intervention.

Finally, there is the theme of "the wasteland," the land
of milk and honey that becomes a desert. The wasteland is
the land where transformations fail to occur. It would be
hard to overstate the crucial significance the "wasteland"
theme has had in philosophical thought. Much of Western
philosophy from the pre-Socratics through Plato and Aristotle has been concerned with humanity's inability to deal
with a world of change or transformations and a desire for
a world outside the domain of change. This theme has
played an equally important role in patriarchal religious
philosophy. Faced with barrenness, patriarchal religion has
dealt with inevitable fate by denying its inevitability and
claiming that its fate was freely chosen. This approach has
examples in the psychological sphere—the mere threat or
fear of an ill fate can bring about a resigned "choice," as in
the case of a prisoner awaiting trial who hangs himself in
his cell. Since men are external to and unable to control the
transformations upon which they are utterly dependent, the
wasteland has been cast as a desired state. Thus, patriarchy
negates the transformation mysteries of earth and woman
(motherland and home) and chooses instead exile and wandering. The conflict, then, is between those who feel at
home in this world, who "put down roots" and rely upon
the fulfillment of the transformation mysteries, and those
who feel estranged from this world, and so as pilgrims

must wander this earth, seeing in their wandering their spiritual destiny. It is against this background that the stories of Cain and Abel, the calling forth of Abraham, the exile of Jacob, and the final exile of the Children of Israel must be understood.

Nomad and Settler

The first conflict in the Bible between settling and nomadism is contained in the story of Cain and Abel. Cain is a farmer; he has literally "put down roots." Abel, the shepherd, is a nomad. Both make offerings to God, but for an unexplained reason Cain's is rejected. Cain then slays Abel, and from the juxtaposition of the events surrounding the murder, one is led to believe that Cain acted out of jealousy. Surprisingly, however, there is a hiatus in the text just where the motivation for the murder might have been revealed. The Hebrew Masoretic text breaks off after the words, "Cain said to his brother Abel"—and picks up with "And when they were outside Cain set upon his brother Abel and killed him."[4] The Samaritan, Septuagint, and other ancient versions supply "Let us go outside" as the missing text,[5] which solves no more than the grammatical problem. Two different interpretations suggest themselves. The first concerns what the murder of Abel may have meant if this first fratricide is regarded as having been adopted from some other tradition. The second suggests what this story meant to practitioners of a patriarchal religion.

S. H. Hooke suggests that the story of the murder of Abel is really the story of a ritual murder for the sake of the renewed fertility of the soil.[6] Cain, the farmer, interprets the rejection of his offering as a forecast of crop failure. In hopes of avoiding it, Cain must perform an expiatory ritual. Since the transformation mysteries are blood mysteries, blood is needed to renew fertility. Ritual is a much more plausible motive for the murder of Abel than jealousy. There are no antecedent events that would support the jealousy theory. Neither is there anything in Cain's sacrifice that would explain or justify its rejection. It is, however, the rejection of Cain's sacrifice that precipitates the murder, and the relationship of Abel's blood to the soil is explicitly mentioned: "Hence you are banned from the soil which forced open its mouth to take your brother's blood from your hand."[7]

More needs to be said about this ritual. In early matri-archal societies, women did the planting and were responsible for the fertility of the soil. Women represented the earth and the earth was female, so fertility depended upon the innate natural sympathy of the human mother to mother earth. When men took over agriculture, they had no innate sympathy with the transformation mysteries. In consequence, they used external sacrifice in an attempt to control something they could neither understand nor partic-ipate in, hence the sacrifice of Abel. The Jewish recounting of this myth is entirely different. The soil, for whose fer-tility the original sacrifice had been offered, is forbidden to Cain and the entire story, though taking place in an agricultural setting, is viewed in a patriarchal nomadic light. What might be considered Cain's sacrifice is treated as Cain's crime and, significantly, his punishment is to become a "restless wanderer on earth." His real crime against patriarchy had been to be a settler and this is corrected by God's judgment.

The conflict does not end there, however. Everything that supports the settler's way of life, including systems of measurement and walled cities which ended mankind's simplicity, springs from Cain's line. All Cain's descendants are eventually destroyed in the Flood. Noah and his sons are descended from Seth, Adam and Eve's third son.

Measurement is attacked throughout the Old Testament. Census-taking, for example, invariably leads to the death of large numbers of people. It is always associated with God's wrath. A pronounced antipathy for walled cities is demonstrated throughout the Old Testament. The city is a symbol of the feminine and the Old Testament itself speaks of cities as women. Cities take on their feminine connotations by being enclosed and protecting. They are frequently built around a "round," a symbol for the womb. Walls are similarly feminine and are rooted in the mother earth from which they spring, hence the expression "I am a wall" in the Song of Songs. A walled city stirs up all the anxieties aroused by female symbols in a patriarchal society. Not only is the founding of cities attributed to Cain, but the inherent evil of cities is demonstrated in the story of the destruction of Sodom and Gomorrah. Nimrod, carrying on Cain's role of villain, was not only a builder of cities, but chief builder of the Tower of Babel.

Sin of Cities

Like the story of Cain and Abel, the account of the construction and succeeding events at Babel is incomplete.
Much is left unsaid and the most important silence relates
to the nature of the sin at Babel. The story, which comprises
just nine sentences in Genesis, describes a world with one
common language. A group of people decided to build a
city and a tower. The Lord saw what they were doing and
confounded their speech, multiplied their languages, and
scattered the people over the entire face of the earth.[8]
Judaeo-Christian tradition explains that God's anger was
caused by the building of a tower meant to storm the heavens. Not only is there no textual support for this tradition,
but the building of towers in the Babylonian tradition was,
on the contrary, a sacred task, designed to facilitate com-
munication between the heavens and the earth.

An examination of God's judgment meted out to the
people of Babel sheds light on the nature of the crime. The
judgment was two-fold: the confusion of language, so that
one people became many; and the dispersion of the people.
If one assumes that the purpose of the judgment was corrective, then it becomes apparent that the crime at Babel
was the crime of building cities.

What is wrong with cities is not merely that they are
matriarchal but that they exemplify "being at home in this
world." People who build cities are putting down roots,
settling, and making claim to more than a wanderer's existence. Babel is a particular affront to patriarchy because
the tower is a monument and in this ephemeral world there

must be no monuments, no lasting transformations. The antipathy toward monuments, or lasting transformations, can be traced through the history of the ark of the covenant. The original ark of the covenant (holding the tablets of the law) was built for travel and was transported in the desert with the Children of Israel. When the Children of Israel settled down, the ark of the covenant was given the central position in the Temple at Jerusalem. But even though the Temple was a monument to God, it was destroyed. It was rebuilt but destroyed again and the ark was lost for all time. It is significant that the ark survived the exigencies of desert travel but not settlement. The true ark is not surrounded by costly stone; rather, it is the ark that can go into exile.

The Virtue of Exile

The patriarchal value of nomadism and exile is also exemplified by the first command to Abraham: "Go forth from your native land . . . to a land that I will show you."[9] Abraham is bidden to leave his native soil, the community of his family and cult, for the sake of a promise that he does not, indeed cannot, understand. The God who commands Abraham is not a God of the soil but a God of history.[10] The alien land is defined not only geographically, but also temporally, for it can never be here and never be now that Abraham is at home and settled. The object of Abraham's wanderings is not that of satisfaction, but that he will remain perpetually unsated, hungering for nonmaterial satisfactions. The essential patriarchal position is

to deny being "at home in the human *milieu* . . . [to] feel
that it is necessary and ordained that [one] should be alone,
a stranger and an exile in relation to every human circle
without exception."[11]

Abraham's son Isaac is not permitted to return to his
homeland to find a wife—his father's servant is sent in his
stead. Isaac's son Jacob is forced to flee from his home after
stealing his brother Esau's blessing. It is only after Jacob
is in exile that God is revealed to him. Similarly, God's
revelation to Moses in the burning bush occurs while
Moses is in exile from Egypt, itself a place of exile. Finally,
the entire nation of Israel flees Egypt to wander in the
desert for forty years and it is during this period that the
sacred law is revealed. In the Old Testament, exile is a
spiritual prerequisite for revelation, and wandering is the
spiritual destiny of God's people. This constant emphasis
on wandering and exile is in direct opposition to the matriarchal principles of home, soil, and roots.

It is clear that for the ancient Hebrews wandering is a
spiritual requirement: those who carry the line of the covenant must be nomads; the institution of the city is danger-
ous; when the people do receive a homeland they lose their
spiritual uniqueness by establishing lines of royalty and
taking on the religious practices of their neighbors. But
why is wandering a religious requirement and what is its
full symbolic import for patriarchy? An examination of
some of the elements of nomadic existence shows how they
stand in direct opposition to the basic principle of the earlier matriarchal religion and thus serve to negate it. Wandering itself contrasts with walled cities, soil, and settlement.

But more than the physical condition of nomadism, the patriarchal concept of wandering represents the spiritual condition of exile and misery—it is the impossibility of feeling at home in this world or with these people. This explains why dispersion did not suffice as a corrective punishment at Babel. Language, and with it the perception of reality, had to be splintered and multiplied so that one could never know certainty or feel secure in this world.

Wasteland as Goal

If the swamp is despised for its "promiscuous fertility,"[12] it is the desert, the place where nothing grows, that is the spiritual destiny of the patriarchal God's chosen people. The wasteland is not man's forlorn condition but his goal! The critical concepts are desert, paradise, and "becoming." The desert stands counter to agrarian cultures in which matriarchy flourished. The fertility rites of matriarchal religions "tempted" all who depended on the fertility of the soil. It was during prayers for rain that the Hebrews called upon the Canaanite god Baal,[13] and it was at the time for sowing that the excesses of orgiastic fertility rites occurred.[14] Agricultural society encouraged such pagan rituals. In the barren desert, on the other hand, the mother god is rendered barren, her rites neglected. The patriarchal god can come to the fore.

The symbolic importance of the desert reaches beyond its anti-agrarian nature. The desert is the domain of the unremitting sun, a patriarchal symbol. The desert sun is not the tool of agriculture but pure radiance, "blinding in its manifestations." Further, the desert stands in opposition to water, which by association with the birth water and semen is symbolic of maternal creation, another basic matriarchal value.[15] Common to all these elements of the desert experience is their opposition to existence. The desert opposes the god of the soil, the giving god, in favor of the god of pain and transcendence. The desert opposes change or "becoming" in favor of stasis or the philosophical concept of "being." Nothing comes to be in the desert. The transformations central to matriarchy constitute indisputable evidence for patriarchy that this world is not the real world— that is, not real in the sense that it has meaning and value. Reality in patriarchy is not changeable, sometimes one thing, sometimes another; it is forever constant. Therefore, patriarchal religion and philosophy have focused on the changeless. They have negated the transformation mysteries of women and soil by negating the world in which these come to pass. Their eye is on the perfect, the incorruptible and unchanging—the spiritual analog of the material desert.

The distinction, then, between fertility and barrenness, agriculture and desert, and ultimately, between settlement and wandering, rests on the distinction between the view that value can be found in this life and the world of change, and the view that value transcends ephemeral existence in the material world and that the life forces of this world must be negated.

5

The Feminization of Judaism in the Zohar

ALTHOUGH THERE were strenuous efforts to eradicate the matriarchal components in Judaism, they inevitably returned and found a welcome within the mystical branch of Judaism and via that route once again into the mainstream religion.

The Zohar is the major work in Jewish mysticism. It appeared for the first time in the thirteenth century, although the text itself claimed that it had been written considerably earlier. Those claims are now disregarded.[1] It is believed that it was in fact written in thirteenth-century Spain. The book is very obscurely written, difficult to read, with arguments that on occasion do not appear to follow one another, and yet, almost from its first appearance, many Jews considered it the most sacred of sacred books. They took it to their hearts and they found in the Zohar something they had not found in traditional Judaism. When orthodox religion fails to meet the need of a people, an unorthodox religion springs up and compensates for this missing element. A study of the Zohar should tell us what was missing in Rabbinic Judaism. One simple interpretation of the difference between standard or traditional Judaism and the

Judaism of the Zohar is that the first appeals to reason and the other to the emotions. While there is certainly truth to this, it may be necessary to probe more deeply to find out why Rabbinic Judaism tends to be legalistic and the Judaism of the Zohar very spiritual.

The Zohar was important to others besides Jews. Christians of that time studied the Zohar. It was translated into Latin by William Postel, and Pico della Mirandola wrote short theses in Latin about it. Mirandola declared that the Zohar contained elements which are capable of a Christian construction.[2] I suggest that this is true, but not in the sense that he meant it. While he was looking for the doctrines of Trinity, original sin, and Incarnation, what he found were the same components in Judaism that the Greeks had found in Christianity, but which are, again, not in normative Christianity. What they have all found and what has drawn people to the Zohar is something that appeals not to logic, but to emotion: that there is a caring concerned parent figure in the universe.

The Zohar is arranged as a commentary on the first five books of the Bible. It suggests that the Bible must be understood in a far more profound way than its simple literal sense. "Woe unto those who see in the Law nothing but simple narratives and ordinary words! . . . The narratives of the Law are but the raiment in which it is swathed. Woe unto him who mistakes the raiment for the Law itself!"[3] One of the major teachings of the Zohar is that the world is an image of the Divine. Carrying this even further, it suggests that the human organs and limbs reflect certain characteristics of God. The Zohar warns us against thinking that man is made up solely of flesh, bones, skin, and sinews (just as the Bible is not made up solely of narratives and words). If the world is an image of the Divine, so is the human body: "Man's skin typifies the firmament, which extends everywhere and covers everything. His flesh typifies the evil side of the universe, i.e. the elements which are purely exterior of sense [reason]. The sinews and veins symbolise the 'Celestial chariot' (the *Merkabah*), being the interior forces of man which are the servitors of God."[4] The Zohar's emphasis on the body is matriarchal—here the body is reclaimed and exalted as a metaphor of the cosmos.

Most significantly of all for matriarchy, in dealing with God's relationship to the world and to humanity, the metaphor is sexual. Man's intimacy with God is the union of male and female. The worlds above are married to the worlds below. Man, who tries to inhabit all these different worlds in his striving after God, shares in cosmic acts of intercourse. This sexual metaphor, as we shall see, is all-pervasive, even down to accounting for the letters used in writing the Bible. Throughout the Zohar a female component is identified—and identified on each level. On the second day of creation there is the separation of the waters. The upper waters are characterized, after separation, as male, and the lower waters as female. On the next day, there is a certain flow or direction to the upper and lower waters so that they should meet in one place in a kind of sexual union, the result of which is to enable the earth or dry land to appear. What is at stake is more than dry land —it is land that would be fertile and would in its turn bring forth life. Again the metaphor is sexual and the relationship of male to female. A sexual metaphor is matriarchal because it returns to the concept of creation from the body and not "by word alone."

Male and Female, Right and Left, Upper and Lower

There are three pairs of ordinary correlative terms used in an extraordinary way in the Zohar. The pairs are: male and female; right and left; upper and lower.[5] The concepts "male" and "female" are used throughout the Zohar in several different senses. First, as a generative pair, that is, whenever one imparts and another receives, the former is called "male" and the latter "female." Second: God's attributes are divided into "male" and "female." For example, wisdom is "male" and understanding is "female." Finally, the whole of creation itself is understood in terms of the sexual model, beginning with the union of God the father and God the mother and carrying a chain of holy intercourse which is completed with the union of the first human couple. This chain, more specifically, is that God "the father" imparts the plan or design of creation to God "the mother." The resulting offspring is "the Voice" (the Voice here is meant as the voice in "God *said* let there be light"). "Voice" is no longer a cold logical principle, but the offspring of the union of the father and the mother. The voice, which is understood to be male, combines with the inchoate material (female) to produce the six days of creation. The male and female forces, now taking the form of the upper and lower waters, combine to produce vegetative powers on earth. The chain of holiness is completed in the union of the first human pair. Sex is behind the whole design of the universe and the holiness of God is imparted through the medium of sex.

The second correlative pair, right and left, is used analogously to the concepts of male and female. Different attributes of God are called male or female and are assigned respectively to the right or left side of God. This is a crucial distinction when we realize that the left side has been associated with matriarchy since the time of Isis in Egyptian matriarchy. One pair of attributes especially significant for the mystic understanding of the problem of evil is rigor (or stern justice) and mercy (or compassion). Rigor is female and on the left side; mercy is male and on the right side. The identification of rigor, or unrelenting justice, with the female side has its counterpart in the Greek tradition in the *Oresteia*, where the Furies (female gods) demand stern justice and the male Olympian deities call for mercy. The supreme attribute of God, "Crown," is beyond the division of male and female—it is in the center.[6]

The correlative pair upper and lower is used in the popular sense of the distinction between heaven and earth. It is also used in a more esoteric sense. According to the Zohar, there are six grades of active or creative or controlling forces. The seventh grade is passive, reflecting on the work of the six other grades. It is the self-conscious introspective faculty of Godhood corresponding to the seventh day of creation on which God rested. It stands to the other grades in the same relationship as the moon (which is female) does to the sun (which is male). It is female and therefore the others are male. The world reflected in this moon is the world of the *Shekhinah*, or the world of the Divine Presence of God. "Shekhinah," a feminine gender word, derived from the Hebrew verb *shakhan* ("the act of dwelling"), was used in post-Biblical times to denote the physical manifestation of God's presence. This abstract concept took on a life of its own and became the feminine aspect of God, fulfilling the function of goddess for the Jews. The Zohar's emphasis on the Shekhinah as the feminine element, opposed to the masculine aspect of God, responded to a deep-seated religious need. The Shekhinah became the loving, motherly, suffering, mourning aspect of Deity who went into exile with the people of Israel and would remain with them until the ultimate redemption. It is this female aspect, identified as the lowest grade of Godhood, which is the most important because it is in this aspect that man has a part. The "upper world," although complete in itself, is regarded as lacking its final consummation with the lower.

This concept of union, of sexual consummation, is so central to the Zoharic view of the universe that it comes out even in its analysis of scripture. Since the Bible is considered to be a sacred and perfect text, nothing that occurs in it can be accidental—everything has meaning. So it is a legitimate question to ask, "Why does the Bible begin with this letter rather than that letter?" In the Prologue to the Zohar, each of the letters presents itself to God for the honor of being first in his scriptures. Each, in turn, is rejected. The rejection of the letter *tsadeh* (written צ) is particularly instructive. "O *Tsadeh*, thou art *Tsadeh*, and

thou signifiest righteousness [being the first letter in the
Hebrew word *tsedek*, "righteousness"], but thou must be
concealed, thou mayest not come out in the open so much
lest thou givest the world cause for offense. For thou con-
sistest of the [female] letter *nun* [נ] surmounted by the
[male] letter *yod* [י] (representing together the male and
the female principles). And this is the mystery of the creation of the first man, who was created with two faces (male
and female combined). In the same way the *nun* and the
yod in the *tsadeh* are turned back to back and not face to
face . . . I will in time divide thee in two, so as to appear
face to face, but thou wilt go up in another place."[7] The
same view, that man was originally man-woman, is expressed in Plato's *Symposium,* and is offered as an explanation of why we search for our missing half.[8]

The letter *bet* [ב] is finally chosen as the first letter in
the Bible, ostensibly because it represents the blessings
offered to God, being the first letter in the Hebrew word
berakhah ("blessing"). However, another reason for the
choice, according to the Zohar, is that *bet* is a powerful
symbol of the union of the upper and lower world. *Bet*
stands in this world but points upward to the next.

God Absolute and Personal

The Zohar deals with one of the central problems of religion
in a typically matriarchal way: How can God be both God
of the whole universe and God of the people of Israel, a
particular people? For if God is not especially concerned
with us, God's concern is not reassuring. Arthur Cohen
makes this point most clearly. The story of Job is being per-

formed: "And now the Lord stretches forth his hand to
comfort the beseeching of the Adversary, a child of his no
less than all of you (and that's the trouble with the universe, isn't it—God's sympathy is so general)."[9] The Zohar
attempts to overcome this generality of God's concern by
the metaphor of a dual aspect of God. Insofar as God is
concerned with all the affairs of state (meaning the whole
universe), he is the king. Insofar as God is concerned with
family and household, God is the queen.[10] So that the God
who is concerned with the covenant, and concerned with a
particular people, is known as *Matrona*, or queen.[11] This
queen is pictured as consorting together in wedlock with
the king of the universe. This is not to say that there are
two Gods. There is one and only one God, but this God is
understood to have different aspects. In the aspect of
the God of a particular people, God is queen, Matrona,
Shekhinah, or Community of Israel, all of which are female.
In the role of God of the universe, God is king, the Holy
one blessed be He. The queen, Shekhinah, or Community of
Israel is like the moon reflecting the light of the sun, which
is the king of the whole universe.

What has Jewish mysticism achieved by this elaborate
and obscure schema of the Zohar? First: it kept Judaism
from falling into the "letter which kills," the strict legalism,
the "good works" as opposed to "faith." It allowed for a
God one could personally relate to—a female, caring, concerned God. The God one relates to, the God one knows, is
the Shekhinah, the feminine aspect of God.

Second: it allows for an explanation of the problem of
evil. The problem of evil is now understood to be the result
of a cataclysm which separated the male from the female

aspects of God. Thus, the existence of rigor or stern justice (female or left side), without being tempered by or coupled with mercy and compassion (male or right side), causes evil to enter the world. The mystics understood very clearly that we need both the female and the male aspects of God.

Another way in which they treat the problem of evil is in terms of Adam's sin. Adam's sin was to separate the attributes of the Tree of Knowledge (right side) from the Tree of Life (left side). Through both of them the total attributes of God had been revealed to Adam, but he chose to divide the two, failing to realize that God's unity was within the sphere of life *and* knowledge. He separated the right—the legal, verbal, analytical approach—from the left—the emotional, creative approach. Recent scientific literature has drawn much the same distinction between the left and right lobes of the brain.[12] For the mystics then, the true nature of God consists of good works and faith, male and female.

The goodness and sacredness of the Divine is dependent on the harmonious interaction of all the attributes. Rigor isolated can turn to evil unless tempered by qualities of love and mercy. God must be known and worshipped through all the attributes. Using the Zoharic structure of the attributes of God, we can now see how the mystics make sense of the story of the sacrifice of Isaac. The story has been understood as an attempt to "prove" Abraham, but the Zohar sees it as an attempt to *improve* him. God sets out to perfect Abraham's character through Isaac in order that the line of the patriarchs may be completed by the eventual appearance of Jacob. At the beginning of the passage, Abraham has not attained perfection, which is the union of all the attributes. (Man is a reflection of God; therefore the attributes of God are also the attributes of man.) Abraham possesses mercy (the male attribute), but he does not possess the quality of rigor (the female). (Or, from our way of looking at it, the Zohar has confused the characteristics of matriarchy with the characteristics of patriarchy.) If he continues in this imperfect state of his soul, the line of the patriarchs will not be completed, and Jacob will not appear. Thus God sends emissaries of rigor to instill Abraham with the necessary quality. Satan tells God that Abraham will not be perfected unless he exercises rigor against Isaac. God allows Abraham to be proved. Isaac, who we are told is thirty-seven at the time of the sacrifice, already possesses rigor and, realizing that his father needed to be perfected, allowed himself to be an instrument for the future of Israel. "On the third day Abraham sighted the place from afar"[13] is understood by the mystics to mean in the third generation (the generation of Jacob). "Isaac broke the silence and said to his father Abraham, 'Father!' "[14] Here Abraham's compassion had been transmuted into rigor, for he approached his son as he would approach an enemy. "But an angel of Yahweh called to him from heaven, 'Abraham! Abraham!' "[15] Because there are two "Abrahams," it is interpreted that his character had become different. The latter is not like the former because Abraham had been perfected.

So the story, that in its traditional formulation meant the triumph of patriarchy, in the mystical understanding meant the reunification of the duality of masculine and feminine.

6

The Cult of Mary

THE JEWISH mystics reintroduced a matriarchal component in Judaism. Christianity gave a shape and form to the feminine aspect through its emphasis on Mary. Just as the Shekhinah took on the role of goddess within Judaism, Mary served the same role for Christianity.

Four characteristics have been shared by the major goddesses of all matriarchal religions:

1. The goddess is the mother of god.[1] Mother of god implies not only temporal priority, but also the special relationship of the goddess to the male god as source of being, consolation, and protection.

2. The goddess is the bride of god.[2] The term "bride of god" represents a much more active relationship to the male god than simply being a passive receptacle for his seed. The relationship includes courtship and love, and serves as a heavenly exemplar for human matrimonial relationships. The same goddess is both mother and bride of the same male god. This is possible because within the religion the male god has a childhood and grows to adulthood. It is then that the goddess who preceded him becomes his bride.[3]

3. The goddess is a virgin. The nature of this virginity is not consistent with the usual understanding of the term, but is compatible with being ravished by the gods, shedding

hymenal blood, and bearing children. For example, Persephone, daughter of Demeter, is ravished by Pluto, sheds hymenal blood from which a pomegranate tree grows, and bears a son; yet she is still called *Kore*, the maiden or virgin.[4] It encompasses an essential purity which cannot be touched by the exigencies of external fate.[5]

4. The goddess mourns her dead. Whether it is Demeter mourning Persephone, Isis mourning Osiris, or Ishtar mourning Tammuz, the concept of *mater dolorosa*, or grieving mother, is part of a complex relationship between the goddess and death. If the goddess is the source of all that is and death is a reality, then she is ultimately responsible also for death. But that responsibility empowers her to mitigate its effect. The dead are buried in the goddess earth, and since the transforming powers are there, what was once alive can live again. Believers in the goddess are assured of overcoming death, so it is she who is sought at the hour of death.

In addition to these four characteristics, certain functions and symbols attach themselves to the concept of goddess in an almost archetypal way: she is the source of salvation, the queen of heaven, the vessel from which all life flows, and the source of all sustenance. She gathers mankind under her sheltering cape and nourishes mankind through the gift of agriculture.[6]

Two great mysteries intrinsic to matriarchy are formulated: the goddess has three identities while remaining one and the female goddess produces a divine male child. The theme of the first mystery is that the goddess appears in three distinct metamorphoses: virgin, mother, and old woman. She is frequently represented as three distinct goddesses and called by three separate names. The mystery is that she is one. This mystery is first understood through worship of the moon, the sacred symbol of the goddess. As the moon each month passes through the three phases of human life—waxing, full, and waning—yet remains always one, so the goddess herself appears as maiden, mother, and old woman, yet always remains one.[7]

With regard to the second mystery, not only is the virgin born of the mother in an ever-renewing cycle, but the male is also born of the female. The goddess recognizes the god she bears as an aspect of herself, born from herself. The second great mystery, then, is that the male arises out of the female and completes her.[8] The corollary of this mystery, that male and female are not antithetical, is a very real human insight.

People have everywhere and at every time had a need for a divine female to worship along with a divine male. From time to time, patriarchal religious doctrine has attacked the concept of a divine female and suppressed her worship. But no sooner was goddess worship beaten back than it reappeared with renewed vitality. The early Near-Eastern religions were replete with goddesses.[9] After the male gods came to the fore, the presence and original priority of the goddesses left traces throughout the sacred texts.[10] Judaism, arising within this context, took special pains to eradicate goddess worship, but, as Raphael Patai convincingly proves,[11] to no avail. The outcry raised against goddess worship by the prophets[12] shows with what tenacity the Hebrews held on to the practice, whether they expressed faith in the neighboring Canaanite goddesses, in their own cherubim, in the feminized "Sabbath Bride," or in the Shekhinah.

Mary as Goddess

It is not surprising that the church expended great efforts to stress that Mary, mother of Jesus, was mortal and merely a receptacle for the Holy Spirit. It is also not surprising that the efforts failed, and one after another, the characteristics of goddesses became associated with Mary. The role of Mary is treated sparsely in the New Testament—the virgin birth is described only in Matthew 1:18 and Luke 1:26. Elsewhere, even in these same two Gospels, Jesus is referred to as the son of Joseph or as the carpenter's son, negating the virgin birth. Neither the Acts nor the Epistles refer to the doctrine, and two early Christian theologians specifically denied it. Cerinthus maintained that Jesus had a natural birth and that the bestowal of supernatural powers coincided with the descent of the Holy Spirit at the time of his baptism.[13] Marcion negated the role of Mary even more strongly by denying that she was the mother of Jesus at all. According to his doctrine, Jesus descended from heaven in the fifteenth year of Tiberius, when he first appeared in the synagogue of Capernaum.[14] Both these positions were declared heretical and Mary's motherhood and virginity became official church doctrine. Nevertheless, there was an uneasy tension between recognizing the role of Mary and keeping it from overwhelming that given to her son, a phenomenon that actually occurred in the Middle Ages.

One attempt, then, to restrain the goddess characterization of Mary was to deny her the first attribute of goddess: that of mother of god. Another attempt was to denigrate the role of corporeal mother. Jesus is quoted as saying, "Who are my mother and my brothers? Whoever does the will of God is my brother, and sister, and mother."[15] In other words, a physical relationship to Christ conveys no special privilege nor any exclusive blessedness. Again, "Blessed is the womb that bore you and the breast that you sucked!" is corrected by Jesus to "Blessed rather are those who hear the word of God and keep it!"[16]

The *Apocryphal Gospels*, condemned by the Apostolic Constitutions as "poisonous," fasten on the infancy of Christ—about which there was a great curiosity but little text—and magnify the role of Mary.[17] Mary is said to emit a light more glorious than the sun, trees bow down to offer their fruits to her, and the sick are healed by being sprinkled with water in which she washed her child.

The second characteristic of a goddess, that she is the bride of God, began to be attributed to Mary in the early Middle Ages. The famous prayer, *Te Deum Laudamus*, includes the lines "All the earth doth worship thee, Spouse of the Eternal Father." Saint Peter Damian, the eleventh-century cardinal and Doctor of the Roman Catholic Church, maintained that when the Virgin Mary matured, she possessed such charm and beauty that God, filled with passion for her, sang the *Canticles* in her praise and that subsequently she became the golden couch upon which God, tired out by the doings of man and angels, lay down to rest.[18] A medieval German discussion on Mary as mother of God explains that Mary's role as bride was necessitated by the fall of Adam; that prior to the fall, the human soul was the bride of God, but after the fall, God's only human bride was the Immaculate Virgin Mary. "When our Father's joy was darkened by Adam's fall, so that He was enangered, the everlasting wisdom of Almighty God was provoked. Then the Father chose me as bride that He might have something to love; because His noble bride the soul was dead. Then the son chose me as mother and the Holy Spirit received me as friend. Then was I alone the bride of the Holy Trinity."[19] This concept of the bride of God as comfort and healer necessitated by the rift between God and mankind is close to the concept of the Shekhinah in Jewish mysticism.

The third characteristic of goddesses attributed to Mary is the special virginity compatible with childbearing. She bears not only Jesus to God, but several other sons and daughters to her earthly husband, Joseph. Mary as virgin became an example for those taking vows of celibacy, attempting to live a life in imitatio Dei. Virginity was important because it made possible a special closeness to God. Furthermore, being born of a virgin mother was often part of the folk history of the hero or savior. Heracles (as hero), Pythagoras (as mystic), Plato (as philosopher), Alexander and Augustus (as emperors), and Buddha (as savior) were all said at one time or another to be products of virgin birth.[20]

Mary's chaste example was also behind the code of chivalry, according to which the lady's honor was defended on pain of death. As the concept of Mary became universalized, all women took on some aspect of her deification. The principle behind chivalry was that each knight was a defender of the cross and each truly loved lady was an example of Our Lady. As such she was adored, though not physically loved, an attitude reflected in medieval poems of courtly love.

The fourth important attribute of the goddess, characterizing her as the mother mourning her dead, is attached to Mary as well. According to the Gospels, Mary is taken away from the scene of the Passion of Jesus before the descent from the cross. When Joseph of Arimathaea takes Jesus down from the cross, the Virgin Mary is not present, although Mary Magdalene and Mary, mother of James and Joseph, are.[21] Nevertheless, the scene of the mourning Virgin Mary, holding the dead body of Jesus, a situation that contradicts Scriptures, has been portrayed in countless works of art. Neumann reproduces art works of many cultures on the theme of the mourning goddess.[22] The parallels between the classic statues of Demeter mourning Persephone, Isis mourning Osiris, Ishtar mourning Tammuz, and Mary mourning Jesus are striking.

The greatest threat to Christian doctrine, as it was originally understood, was the idea that Mary could be the source of salvation. Not only was that Christ's role, it was the whole meaning of his incarnation and sacrifice. Yet more and more, the followers of Mary turned to her both as mediator and as the actual source of salvation. The fourteenth-century English theologian, John Wycliffe, writes: "It seems to me impossible that we should obtain the reward without the help of Mary. There is no sex or age, no rank or position, of anyone in the whole human race, which has no need to call for the help of the Holy Virgin."[23] This view was directly challenged by Berquin in sixteenth-century France. He charged that it was wrong to invoke the Virgin Mary in place of the Holy Spirit and to call her the source of all grace or assign her such titles as "Our Hope" and "Our Life," which rightfully belong only to Christ. In part for putting forth this view, Berquin became one of the first Protestant martyrs in Catholic France.

At the same time that Protestant theologians tried to restrict the role of Mary, Roman Catholicism clung to it more fiercely, recognizing in it a humanizing component lacking in the severity of Lutheranism. The concept of *mater misericordiae*, mother of mercy, was put forth not only in praise of the gentleness of Mary, but also in direct opposition to the character of her son. Jesus was portrayed as the embodiment of God's stern justice, the apocalyptic rider, sword drawn, astride a white steed. Luther warned that it was a dishonor to Christ to represent him solely as judge and not also as redeemer, but the dualism of stern God and forgiving *mother* gained in favor. Along with the growing belief in Mary's mercy grew many stories and legends about her power and acts of intercession. One of the most important is the legend of Theophilus, the proto-type of the Faust legend. A priest who has lost a bishopric makes, in his jealousy and anger, a pact with the devil to regain his position. After he is reinstated, he is filled with remorse and for forty days and forty nights prays to the Virgin Mary. She intercedes and releases him from his pact

to die in peace, free from sin. "Through sin our mortal
brother was lost. But being lost, he returned to life through
thee, O holy Virgin."[24] Goethe's treatment of the Faust
legend ends on a similar note. After Doctor Marianus prays
in adoration to the Virgin Queen of Motherhood, the
chorus mysticus proclaims that "Eternal Womanhood leads
us above."[25]

Mary as Queen of Heaven is praised in song and represented in cathedrals where, by the Middle Ages, she has
frequently usurped Jesus' position in the center of the apse.
It is fascinating to trace the increased importance of Mary
as revealed by her place in art. In the first five centuries
A.D., Mary's subordinate position is reflected in her physical subordination in art. She is portrayed in a position that
is not only lower than Jesus, but also lower than the Magi,
and unlike them, she is shown without halo. By the sixth
century, not only has she been elevated to the position of
central figure in a group of apostles, but she alone is shown
with halo, save for Jesus and the angels. The apostles have
been "demoted" to mortal status. The sixth-century cathe-
dral of Parenzo in Istria portrays Mary as the central figure
in the mosaic of the apse. By the ninth century, two
cathedrals built by Pope Paschal I show Mary enthroned
as the Queen of Heaven in the center of the apse.[26]

As the "Madonna of Mercy," Mary shields the saints
and the apostles with her all-embracing cloak. A Madonna
of Mercy portrait attributed to Saint Luke was sent to Pul-
cheria from Jerusalem in 438. It was regarded as a palladium,
a guarantor of protection and safety, and accompanied the
emperor to the battlefield until the capture of Constan-

tinople in 1453.[27] The palladium has a direct precedent in the Greek tradition. The original palladium was a statue of Pallas Athena, which guaranteed the safety of Athens.

Considered in the light of her great cosmological roles, Mary's original role as passive mortal vessel into which the Holy Spirit placed the infant Jesus seems insignificant. But woman as vessel is an ancient symbol going back to the earliest matriarchal cultures and overlaid with the values of these cultures.[28] The concept is a logical extension of the human experience that woman carries the child "within" her and man enters "into" her during the sex act. Woman as vessel is the source of life: within her life is formed, contained, nourished, and discharged. Human beings project this concept of the human body onto the earth as a whole. Under the surface of the earth is the "womb" from which all life springs forth and to which all life returns. It communicates to the upper regions through the *omphalos*, the navel of the earth. Mary, as mother of God, is "the vessel that was found worthy to contain him whom heaven and earth cannot contain because of the vastness of his glory."[29] If heaven and earth cannot contain the vastness of Christ's glory and Mary can, then Mary can encompass within her not only the heavens and the earth, but God himself. It is precisely this heretical idea that is illustrated by the medieval statue *Vierge ouvrante*,[30] which appears to be the familiar representation of the serene mother and child. But the statue opens to reveal God the Father and God the Son contained within her. Mary is the all-encompassing vessel and they are her contents.

Mary, Mother of Mystery

If the two great mysteries of matriarchal religions are not
merely women's mysteries but human mysteries, as suggested earlier, then they ought to appear in some recogniza-
ble form in patriarchal religions as well. The first great
mystery is that the triple goddess is one: that maiden,
mother, and old woman (or waxing, full, and waning) are
different aspects of the same reality. One possible attempt
at adapting the mystery is in relating the three Marys present at the crucifixion, Mary Cleopas, Mary Magdalene, and
the Virgin Mary, to the triple goddess.[31] This misses the
point—the secret is not that there are three goddesses, but
that the three are one. Mary in herself already fulfills the
roles of virgin, mother, and old woman. The enduring
patriarchal adaptation of the three-in-one theme, however,
is in the Christian Holy Trinity, where Father, Son, and
Holy Spirit are mystically united in one "being." It need
not be construed that there was a direct transition from
triple goddess to Trinity, although a precedent for such a
transition exists in the Eleusinian and Cabirian mystery
religions.

   In the Cult of Eleusis, the mystery of the triple goddess
was not openly alluded to and much that is known about it
is deduced from religious art. The major icon that reveals
the mystery depicts Demeter watching as Persephone pours
water into a vessel. Mother, daughter, and seed (that which
enters the vessel) are one. Fortunately the evidence is not
limited to this one icon. Statues within the sanctuary at
Eleusis reveal what is hidden from noninitiates: that Deme-

ter and Kore have the same face. A key text supplies the
missing link, that Rhea, mother of Demeter, is part of
the mystery. This ancient goddess who dwells on high is the
mother of the mother of the savior, much as Saint Anne is
in Christianity. Kerényi has shown the parallel situation in
the Cabirian mysteries. Here the father gives rise to the son
who gives rise to the seed. In this context, the concept of
the masculine source of life is an inversion of the concept
of the feminine source of life. There is a vessel illustrating
the central doctrine of the Cabirian mysteries in terms exactly parallel to those of the Eleusinian icon. The vessel
illustrates a boy pouring into a cist as his father watches.
Kerényi shows that the Cabirian mysteries had a patriarchal formulation of the trinity.[32] The shared essential
truths in both the Eleusinian and the Cabirian mysteries are
that youth gives way to maturity and then old age, that the
old is perpetually renewed, and that the mystery "My progenitor and I are one" is true for all beings.

Interesting as the Cabirian-Eleusinian parallel may be, of
greater importance in relating the triple-goddess and male
trinity themes is that both serve three basic human concerns: (1) the mystery of the three ages of human life,
youth, maturity, and old age; (2) mankind's place within
the realms of heaven, earth, and the underworld; and (3)
how the dead can come to life again. The triple goddess
rules over three domains, heaven, earth, and the underworld, but it was only by the death of Persephone that the
power could extend to the underworld. Similarly, when
Jesus died, he is said to have harrowed hell. The goddess
had to dwell on earth so that she could understand and

have compassion for mortals. Demeter dwelt on earth among the people of Eleusis and blessed mankind with her mysteries. In Christianity, God became incarnate and blessed humanity as well. Finally, there had to be an aspect of the goddess that was forever immortal, dwelling untouched in the highest regions. This was the role of Rhea, represented by the moon, waxing, full, and waning, but always whole. In patriarchy, this is the first person of the Christian Trinity, God the Father.

The relationship of the triple goddess and the Christian trinity to the moon, however, is a complex one. The moon in matriarchy is not itself a deity, but a powerful symbol of the goddess in her three forms, and is a reminder of the awesome promise of resurrection. Resurrection itself is symbolized not by the monthly renewal of the moon, but by the annual midwinter lunar renewal. This follows the winter solstice—when the Great Mother gives birth to the male sun—which stands at the center of the matriarchal mysteries. It is at this point that the mystery of three-in-one leads to the second great mystery, that the female gives rise to the male who completes her. The death of the feminine moon, the dark moon, is identified with its rape by the male underworld, but from this death comes the "new light" or new moon: "The Virgin has given birth: the light grows."[33] The light that is born from the virgin is a different light qualitatively from the light of the moon that bore it and the goddess recognizes both the difference and that its source is within her. Most appropriately, the birth of Christ is marked almost precisely at the time of the winter solstice.

One additional point may help clarify the role of Mary in the patriarchal framework of Christianity. As Freud suggests, there is a basic duality that reflects the contradictory characteristics of things. For example, the protecting, nurturing mother is also the devouring mother and the goddess of life is the goddess of death. If the concept of Mary is to incorporate the full archetype of goddess, it must contain or reflect the notion of evil as well as goodness. This duality is in fact preserved. Mary is regarded to be the other aspect of Eve. The angel's greeting to her, "Ave," is the reversal of the name "Eva."[34] Just as the cross is taken to be the inversion of the Tree of Life, Mary is the inversion of Eve. Eve takes the fruit from the Tree of Knowledge and Mary, through her gift of Jesus, returns the fruit and restores humankind to its sinless state. Eve is the mother of all that lives and Mary is the virgin. Eve symbolizes matter, Mary symbolizes spirit. Finally, through Eve all women are cursed and through Mary all women are blessed.

7

Characteristics of Matriarchal Religions

AS WE HAVE already seen, the difference between the two contradictory models for formulating religion, matriarchy and patriarchy, is far greater than the difference between God the father and God the mother. The difference strikes at the very heart of meaning and value in life. There is an uneasy tension between these two forms of thought—one supplants the other but traces of the earlier form remain.

What are the differences between matriarchal and patriarchal systems? Why are religions structured in these two opposing ways? Why does one form give way to the other? Finally, what needs does each system fulfill for the religious person?

Central to any matriarchal religion is the existence of a female major deity. In keeping with this elevated role in theology, woman's social role in matriarchy is superior: inheritance is determined through the mother, the child carries the mother's name, and it is the mother who chooses the child's given name. The relationship between mother and child creates the primary ethical obligations. The priority of the woman gives rise to the symbolic interpretation of certain concepts, such as settlement and soil, left, the number two, etc.

Within any religious system, these philosophical concerns are of overriding importance: the nature of the deity, the grounding of ethics, the view of the material world, the meaning of death, and the meaning of life. There are, of course, other concerns. The most important, the problem of evil, will be treated in a later chapter and shown to be closely related to the view of the nature of the deity. The nature of creation (innately good or evil) will also be shown to grow out of an answer to this first fundamental question. If we know our source and understand our relationship to it, we have begun to answer many of the other major religious questions. In a sense the formulation of these questions grows out of Freud's analysis of religion. As noted earlier, Freud suggests that religion's concern is threefold: (1) cosmology—where do we come from and in what relation do we stand to our source? (2) consolation—what is the meaning of what we suffer here and where is our suffering leading? and (3) ethics—how ought we to live? While the questions may be put differently or in a different order, clearly all religions do deal with the questions Where do I come from? Where am I going? and How ought I to live here and now?

The ethical question was originally distinct from the religious question—a person could be ritually correct but not necessarily good. Plato is the first in the Western philosophical tradition to assert that God equals good. In the religious tradition, the same point is made when Abraham asserts that the God of Justice should be just. In addition to these fundamental questions, most religions have any number of secondary traits deriving from the particular religion's solutions to these five basic questions. These secondary traits manifest themselves in ritual.

Ritual has been understood in many different ways. Joseph Campbell considers it a form of "play" where if one acts as if the beliefs were held, belief will come.[1] Others have stressed its social function—to show people their roles in society. Either way, the most trivial rituals must be understood to symbolize serious beliefs about reality. In this light, secondary traits manifesting themselves in ritual are seen as the "acting out" of the theory expressed in the theology. Examples would be the sacredness of certain animals, colors, numbers, or times of day, or prohibitions against certain kinds of dress or music.

Six secondary traits will be studied in detail. While these six can be well documented in Old and New Testament sources and their commentaries, they should be viewed only as examples. Many other secondary traits could be studied in the same way, for example, colors, days of the week, planets and constellations, letters of the alphabet, shapes, climate, light and dark, bodily processes, metals, jewels, minerals, hours, loops and bonds, and mountains and valleys. The meaning of animals in religion, for instance, is a fascinating subject in its own right. Each of the New Testament Gospel writers was associated with an animal and all religions designate some animals as especially fit for sacrifice and others as "unclean." In the Eleusinian Mysteries, the pig is identified with the goddess Demeter and is therefore sacred in matriarchy and (perhaps for the same reason) is prohibited in patriarchy. The fish, by association with the goddess Venus, is also sacred in matriarchy. In patriarchy, the fish is identified with Christ through an acronym: the initial letters of the Greek for the words "Jesus Christ, God and Savior" spell out most of the word for "fish." This play on words became a serious metaphor when the acronym was taken to symbolize Christ's role as fisher of lost souls. The identification of Christ and fish also played a role in converting the followers of the matriarchal Eleusinian Mysteries to Christianity.[2] The concept of sacred and profane is extended to include plants as well. Trees have especially rich symbolic import, but certain vines are also revered or disdained in different traditions.

The tabulations on pages 86 and 87 show the five essential categories of opposition in matriarchy and patriarchy, and the six secondary characteristics to be examined.

The symbolic traits and rituals listed in the table manifest themselves in three different ways: some are specifically set forth in religious writings in the context of positive doctrines (as, for example, the importance of the left hand of Isis in the Egyptian religion[3]); others can be clearly identified as vestiges of matriarchy in patriarchal religions (as the Canaanite cult of the goddess Asherah which survived within early Judaism[4]); and still others can be deduced from practices in patriarchy which do not derive from any positive religious doctrine but which become meaningful when seen as injunctions against earlier practices.

The first way is the most direct and most easily supported. The sacredness of the pomegranate is explicitly affirmed and explained in stories attached to the Eleusinian Mysteries; the role of the bull is well attested to in the

Categories of Opposition in Matriarchy and Patriarchy

		Matriarchy	Patriarchy
1. Nature of the deity.	A. B.	God is female. Union of divine female and mortal male to produce superior being.	God is male. Union of divine male and mortal female to produce superior being.
2. Grounding of ethics.		Ethical system based on blood tie.	Ethical system based on abstract principle.
3. View of matter and material world.		Material creation the model for all creation. Reality and value found in the material world.	Reason the model for all creation. Reality and value found in the spiritual world.
4. Meaning of death.		Death terminates material existence, which is the only real existence.	Death is the entry to spiritual existence, which is the highest form of existence.
5. Meaning of life.		Time is cyclical, renewing itself endlessly. Meaning of life found in terms of life itself and contribution to its renewal.	Time is linear, moving toward a goal. Meaning of life found in terms of contribution to the goal.

Selected Secondary Ritualistic Concerns

Matriarchy	Patriarchy
6. Moon and lunar calendar. Night precedes day.	Sun and solar calendar. Day precedes night.
7. Settlement and soil.	Nomadism.
8. Lower.	Upper.
9. Left.	Right.
10. The number two and evenness.	The number one and oddness.
11. The mother names the child and inheritance is through the mother.	The father names the child and inheritance is through the father.

Dionysian cult. Unfortunately, holy writ describes only a few of the many practices and symbols of any faith. The second way traits are identified presents a more difficult approach because theologians are reluctant to admit that their religion has absorbed earlier practices. Comparative religion and archeology offer the best support here. The tirades of Old Testament prophets against certain pagan practices alert us to the fact that the practices were still current among the Jews.

An example of the third type of ritual manifestation is the unexplained injunction in Exodus against boiling a kid in its mother's milk. This was a conscious rejection of the Ugaritic practice of cooking a kid in milk for a ritual meal

in honor of the gods Shahar and Shalim.[5] The Hebrews
were warned not to go inquiring after their (Canaanite)
gods, thus: " 'How did these nations serve their gods?—
that I also may do likewise.' You shall not do so to the
Lord your God; for every abominable thing which the Lord
hates they have done for their gods.'"[6] The same mode of
reasoning explains the patriarchal priority of the sun over
the moon and the right over the left hand. Caution must
prevail in applying this method because while something
may be required in matriarchy and forbidden in patriarchy,
no causal relationship may exist. Moreover, theologians
hold the teachings and practices of their religions to be
divinely inspired and as such, to have positive value in their
own right. For this reason, arguments based on this method
of identification of traits are as unacceptable to the theologian as the previous method. The characteristics of
matriarchal religions listed in the table will now be examined more closely.

God as Female

In a matriarchal religion, the most supreme god, or the god
who always was and who created the other gods, is female.
The female presence is a given; the origin of the male, however, requires explanation in terms of the primordial
female. In particular, the birth and childhood of male gods
is usually documented in the religion's tradition. In the
Sumerian myth on the origin of the universe, the goddess
Nammu is described as "the mother who gave birth to

heaven and earth."[7] In the Babylonian creation story, the goddess Tiamat gives birth to gods and goddesses up to the generation of the god Marduk. Marduk eventually kills her and splits her body in two, creating the sky and the earth.[8] In the Egyptian creation story, Nun, the female primeval ocean, gives rise to Atum, the sun god, who then commences the rest of creation.[9] In the Greek tradition, the earth goddess, Gaea, emerges from what is probably the primal vagina, "the abyss sensing everything." Gaea, while remaining a virgin, creates Uranos, the sky, who is her son.[10]

When it is not the female who is first, it is her symbol, the egg, which gives rise to the rest of creation. The Hindu god Brahma dwells in the original egg and finally divides it into Heaven and earth. The age-old riddle, "Which came first, the chicken or the egg?" is a classic formulation of the conflict between patriarchy and matriarchy. The egg in the riddle represents the externalized womb. To hold that the egg came first is to hold that woman, as prime matter, is the source of life. Choosing the chicken is to reject woman as the source. In this case, the image (the chicken) precedes the matter out of which it is created, or, in Platonic terms, the form (essence or idea) of the bird is prior to the matter. The chicken-egg conflict culminates in the Egyptian myth of the phoenix. In this myth, the magic bird appears and delivers an egg. The egg is placed on the altar of the sun god, who is male. The egg, however, is hollowed out and filled, not with the matter of life, but with the carcass of the phoenix's dead father. The egg is burned on the altar of the sun and the resurrected and rejuvenated father phoenix flies out of the ashes. The symbolic gender of the female egg is directly reversed in this story. Fertilization occurs by fire and the sun gives rise to the father who gives rise to the son, all without female intervention. This process is clearly a negation of the earlier matriarchal primacy of the prime matter or female.

The basic premise of matriarchy is the priority of the female. Priority must be understood in three senses: priority in time, in understanding, and in importance.[11] Priority in time, simply put, means that in the beginning was the woman. This is to be understood in three ways: (1) the creator is female (Nun in the Egyptian myth); (2) the original matter out of which the universe was formed is female (Tiamat the goddess is the matter out of which heaven and earth are formed); (3) creation is by sexual reproduction, a combination of (1) and (2) (the earth goddess Ki in the Sumerian myth unites with An, heaven, and gives birth to Enlil, air[12]).

Priority in understanding means that from the understanding of female creation, which is material creation, all other understanding is derived. We use the material concept of the shaping of unformed matter to explain our structuring of perception. We form it the way a potter would form clay.

Finally, priority in importance signifies that all concepts derived from the female material principle are more important than those from other sources. For example, the material experience of the mother-child relationship yields a more important obligation than a command from an abstract God to "sacrifice your child."

Union of Divine Female and Mortal Male

The union of a divine mother with a mortal father to produce a superior child is frequently found in matriarchal mythologies. Achilles, for example, is the offspring of the goddess Thetis and the mortal Peleus. In the Bible, which is basically patriarchal, the genders are reversed. The first instance is in Genesis 6:2–4, where "the divine beings saw how beautiful were the human daughters and took as their wives any of them they liked. . . . It was then that the Nephilim appeared on earth—as well as later—after the divine beings had united with human daughters [and they bore children to them[13]]. Those were the heroes of old, men of renown."

The New Testament, however, provides a more far-reaching instance. God the Father unites with Mary who nevertheless remains a virgin, to produce Jesus, the incarnation of God. This formulation not only relegates to woman the passive role of receptacle for the divine (male) spirit, but Mary's role is deemed so insignificant that early Christians debated whether Jesus received his divine powers while in the womb (which would have given Mary some significance) or only at his baptism.

Ethical System Based on Blood Tie

The parent-child relationship forms the basis of the entire system of ethical obligations in matriarchy. The conflict between this system and the patriarchal ethic, built on abstract ideas, becomes a prominent theme in Greek tragedy. Orestes faces the contrary obligations of blood tie to his mother and the need to avenge her murder of his father, Agamemnon. Agamemnon, with no qualms about blood ties, had sacrificed his daughter Iphigenia to the gods in order to obtain a favorable wind to sail for Troy.

The story of Jephthah in the Old Testament has a strikingly similar theme. Jephthah, wishing victory in battle, promises God that he will sacrifice the first person to greet him on his return. That person is his only daughter and he duly sacrifices her. The demand to sacrifice one's children to the gods draws out the ethical conflict between matriarchy and patriarchy. The conflict of obligations to one's flesh and one's God helps explain Abraham's offering of Isaac and God's sacrifice of his son in the New Testament.

The obligation in matriarchy, however, is not only parent to child, but child to parent as well. Seen in this context, it becomes clear why the Biblical commandment to "honor your father and your mother" is appended with the explanation "that your days may be long in the land which the Lord your God gives you." The child to parent obligation is included in the code for the child's protection. If parents could not rely on the respect of their grown children, they would have less incentive to care for and nurture them as babies.

In effect the commandment says, "You had better honor your parents so that they will take care of you and you may have a long life." Such a command in matriarchy would be unnecessary because the parent-child relationship constitutes the basic ethical obligation and therefore needs no support or justification. It is the first principle of matriarchy and other principles are justified in terms of it.

Primacy of Material Creation and Material World

Material creation is the creation of something new out of existing matter, as opposed to *creatio ex nihilo*, creation out of nothing. The concept of material creation is the basis for understanding human reproduction. As such it is also, in matriarchal systems, the basis for understanding the creation of the universe, as well as all creation in the universe. The connection between human reproduction and other material creation figured prominently in ancient matriarchal religions. New Year ceremonies of the Babylonians, the Greeks, and even the later Northern Europeans to renew the fertility of the soil featured sacred orgies.[14] In other words, human sexual reproduction was a model for all reproduction and by imitative magic, having sexual relations in the newly planted fields would aid the crops.

The belief in the material creation of the universe occurs throughout early Near-Eastern mythology without exception. The Sumerians, Babylonians, Egyptians, Canaanites, Hittites, and Greeks all understood creation originally in terms of procreation, and only later in terms of fabrication (which still presupposes matter which must be ordered). In Greek myth, Eurynome, Goddess of All Things, rose naked from chaos, divided the sea from the sky, danced upon the waves, stirred up the wind, was impregnated by it in the shape of a great serpent named Ophion, and laid the world egg. In another story from the Greek tradition, Night, the creatrix, lays a silver egg from which Love is hatched to set the universe in motion.[15]

The move away from the concept of material creation can

be traced in the Babylonian creation myth. While originally the world is created out of the body of the slaughtered Tiamat, Marduk's test for divine kingship requires him to create "by word of mouth alone." The Old Testament God creates by word, although there is some ambiguity as to whether it is creation from matter or *ex nihilo*. The question is, What was there "in the beginning" when God created the heavens and the earth—was there nothing, or was there matter which God ordered but did not create? The ambiguity hinges on the translation of the Hebrew words *tohu* and *bohu* applied to the earth in Genesis 1:2. The words are usually rendered "unformed" and "void," but since they occur nowhere else in the Bible, their translation cannot be tested in another context. Graves and Patai postulate an identity of *tohu* with a sea-monster, Tehomet, related to the Babylonian Tiamat, and *bohu* with a land-monster, Behemoth.[16] By the time of the writing of the last of the four Gospels, the ambiguity is gone. John 1:1 begins, "In the beginning was the Word"—material creation had been absolutely discarded. The progression, then, is from a female creator to a male creator who still uses matter, to a complete denial of the material component in creation.

The same three stages are found regarding reproduction. First, as exemplified by the Cult of Demeter, motherhood is primary and the womb is of overriding concern. Later, as in the Dionysian Cult, fatherhood and the phallic principle come to the fore. Dionysianism represents a move away from matriarchy. However, although it stands for the phallic principle as opposed to the womb, Dionysianism still represents the primacy of sex and the importance of material reproduction. The final stage, and the most strongly patriarchal, is exemplified by Apollo, who negates the body and rejects this material world for the Olympian realm. Spiritual creation, celibacy, and rejection of the material world are archetypically patriarchal.

In matriarchy, an understanding of female (i.e., material) creation underlies all other understanding. The understanding of every concept, process, or value judgment begins with the material world, and the idea to be understood is drawn out of this real world. In the question of the chicken and the egg, the stuff of which the chicken is made is needed before an idea of the bird can be formed. The egg-chicken question of material creation *vs.* the primacy of the idea is not only a religious concern but a philosophical and a legal concern as well. One of the greatest conflicts in the history of philosophy is between the positions of Plato and Aristotle. Plato maintains that the idea is prior. He posits, for example, the idea of the good. Then, using an abstract knowledge of the good, a person can look at the world and judge whether or not a specific action, person, or institution is good. Aristotle holds that this material world is prior. From a person's experience in the real world of many good actions he abstracts a concept of goodness. Similarly, when Aristotle explains the building of a house or sculpting of a statue, his model is natural creation, and he asks how nature, if it were a person, would do it.

The matter-idea conflict is brought to bear on law in the writings of the Roman Emperor Julian. In justifying a law on rights of inheritance, Julian uses the model of agriculture to carry his point. "All produce is gathered not according to the right of the seed, but the right of the soil. . . . In gathering fruit, more heed is given to the right of the body from which they are taken, than to that of the seed from which they grow."[17] Therefore the child of a slave woman is a slave. Julian's Roman law has a counterpart in Jewish religious law. The child of a Jewish mother is considered to be Jewish, regardless of the father's religion, and the child of a non-Jewish mother is not Jewish.

Death as the Termination of Existence

The matriarchal view of death is a direct consequence of the reverence for physical, material creation and the material world as a whole. Since material existence is regarded as the only existence, and death terminates material existence, death is regarded as evil. More than that, because the womb and the earth are equated, the mother (earth) is seen as both the source of life and the recipient of the dead. This reinforces the matriarchal mourning of death.[18]

By contrast, death in patriarchy is welcomed as a release from the burden of corporeal existence. This view is typified in Bach cantata texts ("Come, thou sweet hour of death," "Come, sweet death") and is expressed by Plato in commenting on the death of Socrates:

So long as we keep to the body and our soul is contaminated with this imperfection, there is no chance of our ever attaining satisfactorily to our object, which we assert to be truth. . . . It seems that so long as we are alive, we shall continue closest to knowledge if we avoid as much as we can all contact and association with the body, except when they are absolutely necessary, and instead of allowing ourselves to become infected with its nature, purify ourselves from it until God himself gives us deliverance.[19]

The anguish felt at the death of material creation is thus seen to be directly proportional to the value placed on its existence.

Time as Cyclical

The table of categories of opposition lists the nature of time under the question of the meaning of life. The choice of the nature of time, cyclical or linear, determines whether meaning is found in the present process or in some future age. This will become clearer as the two perspectives are examined more closely. An examination such as this is possible because Kant recognized that time is not a fact about the world, but a way of structuring perception and creating reality.[20] This is a difficult and important insight and deserves some clarification. We know that material objects are facts about the world: we see them, trip over them, experience them. But what exactly is time? We do not sense it; we use it to describe, order, and explain other things that we do sense. We watch an egg drop and the yolk shatter. We say that it took six seconds. What were these six seconds? They were not properties of the egg. They are our way of measuring the process of before (the egg landed) and after (the egg landed). So time must be considered as a mental construct which helps us to understand and order our world, but does not itself exist in the world. Mental constructs and Kant's view will be discussed further in the next chapter.

Time has been identified as cyclical or linear in nature, depending on the orientation of the society that defined it. Cassirer and Eliade have determined that in earlier societies the concept of time was cyclical, that is, based on the fact that every year the earth produces life, every year it dies, and every year it renews itself.[21] This eternal recurrence is the framework within which human events take place.

The cyclical concept is rooted in matriarchal tradition both historically and, more important, ideologically. The matriarchal recognition of kinship with the material world leads to an interpretation of time based on the observation of significant worldly events. In an agricultural society, these events are almost exclusively cyclical. Both the earth and its cyclical nature are mirrored in the female menstrual cycle, hence the overwhelmingly feminine identification of cyclical time.

In matriarchy, not only is the cyclical nature of time identified, it actually serves as the source of meaning in life. Value lies within the process of life itself and is derived from life by means of paradigms. A paradigm may be thought of as a timeless model of an event. A particular human event, then, is regarded as an instance of the paradigm. It possesses meaning and indeed can only be understood insofar as it fulfills the paradigm. This helps to explain the presence, as pointed out by Freud, Rank, Eliade, and others, of an archetypal "hero" story in widely separated cultures.[22] In the story, the hero has an obscure or supernatural birth, is drawn from water, is abandoned by his parents, overcomes great trials, and finally reaches his rightful estate. If a real person is regarded as a hero, his biography must conform to the paradigm. Insofar as it does not, it is replaced by the mythical biography which clearly identifies the person as hero.

The central factor of the cyclical view of time, eternal recurrence, dominates the Old Testament book of Ecclesiastes —"For everything there is a season," "There is nothing new under the sun," etc. Recurrence is held to imply changelessness and to preclude evolution and progress. Thus, based on the same matriarchal premise of the cyclical nature of time, Ecclesiastes derives the diametrically opposite conclusion that life is vanity—in other words, things just happen over and over again, without any meaning or purpose. This view rules out teleology, the belief that the universe is designed for a purpose and that things are working toward an end. To accommodate teleology, time must be regarded as progressing historically, or linearly, from a beginning toward some end of days. Value in such a system lies in furthering and finally achieving the goal (for example, the Messianic age or the Apocalypse). The patriarchal Judaeo-Christian religion is fundamentally teleological, with time regarded as linear. The heavy overlay of cyclical ritual, which can be considered a matriarchal remnant, is itself engulfed in the teleology. Reenacting on Good Friday the pain and suffering of Jesus on the cross partakes of the paradigm of the Passion. The purpose of doing so, however, is less to find meaning for suffering than to bring about the kingdom of heaven on earth for all.

Cyclical time is based on the observation that things re-

cur: the soil brings forth fruit, lies bare, and then once
again brings forth fruit in an unending pattern. The linear
view of time is also based on an observation—that certain
processes are unidirectional. The egg is dropped and the
yolk shattered but once, in a process that is not reversible.
The linear view sees time as moving relentlessly toward
some final goal.

The distinction between cyclical and linear time cannot
be drawn empirically because each view has an empirical
basis. In any case, time itself is not an empirical fact about
the world, but a mental tool through which people understand the world. Therefore, the concept of linear time cannot be considered a "discovery" such as the earth's being
spherical, but must be regarded as an interpretation based
on ideology. (Friedrich Nietzsche, for example, advocated
cyclical time on ideological rather than scientific grounds.)
Patriarchal culture stresses alienation from this imperfect
physical world and fosters a Messianic goal of release to a
purely spiritual existence. This can only be achieved within
a framework of linear time.

In the same way that the distinction in time is drawn between the matriarchal, where one is immersed in this world,
and the patriarchal, where one seeks the spiritual realm,
Wilhelm Worringer draws a distinction between a three-
dimensional and a two-dimensional view of space.[23] Although there is nothing analogous to a calendar with regard
to space, the view of space can be derived from the art of
the culture involved. Worringer saw a direct relationship
between the culture's view of the world and the artist's
treatment of depth and perspective. In a society where one

is immersed in the material world, space and depth are treated with great emphasis. Renaissance paintings, for example, representing the art of a humanistic culture, feature foreground arches and distant panoramas frequently irrelevant to the subject matter of the painting. The art of life-denying societies, on the other hand, or societies focused on an end of days, lacks depth and perspective, for example, Egyptian, medieval European, and twentieth-century abstract art. This is not because of any defect in the artists' techniques. On the grounds of the underlying cultural ideology, the spirit (essence or form) is abstracted from its physical context. Similar distinctions might be drawn between harmonic and polyphonic structuring of music, between styles of architecture, between forms in literature, and in other areas of human endeavor.

SECONDARY CHARACTERISTICS

The Moon and Lunar Calendar

Two other distinctions between matriarchy and patriarchy relating to time are the reckoning of time by the lunar or the solar calendar and the relative importance of night and day. In matriarchy, the moon has priority over the sun; it is considered to be a female goddess associated with the night, while the sun is largely ignored. Even the plants are believed to regulate their growth according to the moon. In actual matriarchal practice, sowing was adjusted to lunar phases and the moon cycles were used to fix the times for customs, assemblies, festivals, and divisions of the year. Nighttime was preferred for meetings and councils.[24]

Compromises of varying degrees between the lunar and solar calendars are reached in the Judaeo-Christian tradition. Moslems use a religious calendar comprised of twelve lunar months. Although this is as close as one can get to the solar year by which the seasons on earth are determined, it still falls short by some eleven days. As a result, the celebration of the feast of Ramadan may occur in the spring of one year and in mid-winter eight years later. Jewish calendar time is reckoned by the moon and marked by monthly prayers on the occasion of the new moon, but the calendar is adjusted to the solar year by the insertion of a leap month every two or three years. An additional element used in determining the length of certain Jewish months is the seven-day week cycle.

The church calendar is an annually adjusted lunar calendar superimposed on a solar calendar, but also influenced by the weekly cycle. The underlying solar calendar determines the fixed feasts, such as All Saints Day on November 1 and Christmas on December 25. The movable feasts, such as Palm Sunday and Pentecost, are determined by the date of Easter. Easter Day is fixed each year as the first Sunday (weekly influence) after the first full moon (lunar calendar) following the spring equinox (annual adjustment to solar calendar).

The historical connection between the events of Paschaltide and the Jewish Passover provides the rationale for the unusually involved method of fixing the date of Easter. It does not, however, explain the tenacity with which the lunar calendar principle has survived in the face of mankind's contrary experience with the solar seasons. An answer to this question may lie in man's view of the moon as goddess and as symbolic of earthly material existence, particularly female existence. The lunar phases of waxing, full, and waning are identified with the three feminine ages of virginity, motherhood, and old woman. This identification is strengthened by the connection between the lunar and menstrual cycles.

Related to the lunar principle are the concepts of darkness and night. Night is considered feminine in matriarchy, not only through its association with the moon, but also because it is thought to give birth to day. A compromise between night and day is worked out in the Zohar. The Sabbath, dejected, comes before the Lord and complains, "O Lord of the universe, since the time when Thou didst create me, I have been called merely '*day* of Sabbath' [italics mine], but surely a day must have for companion a night." The Lord agrees with the Sabbath and confers upon it "an even more glorious crown" that the *eve* of the Sabbath should inspire fear.[25]

Soil, Settlement, and Cities

In matriarchy, agriculture in all its aspects is a sacred practice requiring special rites at the plowing of the field (traditionally done by males and held to be analogous to marriage), at the sowing of the seed, and at harvest, where first fruits are reserved for ritual offering. The knowledge of agriculture is viewed as a divine gift to mankind and the donor is traditionally a goddess.

Through the furtherance of agriculture, women are also seen as founders of settlements. In matriarchal tradition, not only crops spring from the ground, but also the walls that guard cities. The walls are said to spring from the very womb of the earth and in earlier times they were hallowed in strict rites.[26] It was their relationship to the maternal god that granted protection, not their physical strength. The Old Testament story of Joshua at the walls of Jericho exemplifies the conflict between matriarchy and patriarchy. The matriarchal walls are destroyed by the blasting of the phallic rams' horns.

The patriarchal religions cling to the tradition of nomadism and for them the founding of cities always marks the prelude to disaster: a decline from spirituality or a return to earlier gods.

Primacy of Lower

In patriarchal religions, God, if he is not in the highest heavens, is at least atop a mountain, such as Olympus or Sinai.[27] In matriarchy, where God is identified with the earth, one descends to address the gods. In the Greek religion, it is where the earth is cleft apart that oracles come forth. Temples arise from those places and are holy because of what is beneath them, not because of what they rise toward. Even Delphi, the major stronghold of the male, spiritual god, was built around the ancient navel stone of

the earth goddess, Gaea. When Oedipus is called to his final
reward at the end of *Oedipus at Colonus,* he is not gathered
up into a cloud, but rather "the foundations of the earth
split open to take him without pain. . ."[28] The only textual
trace of the holiness of the "lower" in the Judaeo-Christian
tradition is found in Jewish mystical texts which refer to
going "down before the ark [of the temple]" and which in-
terpret Psalm 130:1, "Out of the depths I cry to you," to
mean that God is in these depths. But while Judaism does
not recognize the sacredness of the lower realm generally, a
sense of sacredness does affect the choice of holy sites.
Jerusalem is described in Ezekiel 38:12 as being *tabur
ha-arets,* the navel or center of the earth, a concept identical
with the Greek concept of *omphalos.*

Once the categories "upper" and "lower" are identified as
patriarchal or matriarchal, value judgments based on these
concepts quickly follow. In patriarchy the non-judgmental
terms "upper" and "lower" lead to such evaluative terms as
high/low, rise/fall, climb/stoop, superior/inferior, ele-
vated/cast down, look up to/look down on.

Primacy of Left

Ethnologists are agreed that left corresponds to the feminine side and right to the masculine. In the Egyptian religion, it is the left hand of Isis which restores Osiris. In
Islam, despite its being a patriarchal religion, the left hand
of Fatima (daughter of the prophet) is carried in procession.
In the Greek religion, when Aphrodite helps Theseus, he
rewards her by building an altar on the left side of a moun-

tain and decorating it with left horns. The sons of Pelopides, who wanted to show their maternal lineage, wore the Gorgon's head on their left shoulders. Amazon women are described as having cut off their right breasts to remove any masculinity in them. Finally, Jewish folk tradition relates that at the time of the flood, the cat had not yet been created. Noah's ark quickly became overrun with mice, and so the lion snorted forth two cats—from the right nostril a tomcat, and from the left, a female.

Why is left considered matriarchal and right patriarchal? Two different reasons can be offered. The first has to do with the location of the heart on the left side. Mothers, whether right-handed or left-handed, "instinctively" tend to hold their babies with their heads to the left side, where the soothing sound of the heartbeat is located. A study of works of art portraying Madonna and child shows that in periods of naturalism and realism, the Madonnas are portrayed holding the child on the left side; in the medieval period, the child is as likely to be held on the right side.[29]

The second reason for the identification of left with matriarchy and right with patriarchy is connected with the difference between the left and right sides of the body (especially the hands) and their controlling lobes of the brain. Roger Sperry has empirically mapped out the controlling functions of the lobes of the brain, confirming a distinction between the left and right side of the body that appears in earliest mythology.[30] To the left side of the body belong dreams, the unconscious, the non-verbal, the creative; to the right belong the verbal, rational aspects of humanity. Identification of the female with the left brought with it the view that artists were effeminate and women could not (and should not) study philosophy because of their emotional and irrational nature.

Symbolism of left for female and right for male appears in early architecture. The entrance columns of Solomon's temple and of the legendary temple of Hercules at Tyre are asymmetrical. Marc Saunier regards the right and left columns as representing evolution (masculine) and involution (feminine), good and evil, or the Tree of Life (masculine) and the Tree of Knowledge of Good and Evil, i.e., sexual knowledge (feminine).[31]

The Number Two and Evenness

Number symbolism is found throughout the world with a remarkable agreement as to what the numbers symbolize. Before numbers were understood to be abstract representations of quantity, they were considered as powerful mystical symbols of the forces in the cosmos. For the Pythagoreans, the number "two" stood at the beginning of the numerical series just as woman stood at the summit of the material world. "Two" allows for a differentiation between even and odd while "one" admits of no differentiation. "One," which comes before differentiation, is pure spirit and gives to "oddness" its spiritual cast. "Two" is the symbol of the coupling of male and female, hence it represents the material world. This gives to "evenness" its matriarchal importance.

"Three" is the result of the union of "one" and "two." It contains matter, but transcends it and resolves the con-

flict between "one" and "two," spirit and matter. The
Trinity can be examined in terms of this numerological
symbolism. The first member of the Trinity is God the
Father, who is the Almighty Spirit. The second member of
the Trinity was *begotten*, made *incarnate*, suffered, and was
buried (the end of all matter). The third member, the Holy
Ghost, "who proceedeth from the Father and the Son"
("one" and "two"), remained with the bereaved disciples
to comfort and instruct them until the second coming of
Christ.

"One" is understood as pure spirit, "two" as matter. In
any given culture, however, whether these are evaluated
as good or evil depends upon the view of the material world
held by that culture. In patriarchal religions, "two" is seen
as ominous, representing conflict, struggle, and inner dis-
integration. In matriarchal religions, "one" is considered to
be defective and "two" is seen as an advance from unity
to the duality of the sexes manifested in material creation.
In the Zohar, "one" is seen as complete in itself but less
perfect than "two," which is united for consummation.

Mother Names Child

Herodotus reports that the people of Lycia take their names
from their mother and not from their father: "For when one
asks a Lycian who he is, he will indicate his descent on his
mother's side, and list his mother's mothers."[32] Together
with the name, status comes through the mother's lineage.
As important as the family name and status are, however,
the given name is also important. Its selection has always

been made with great care, frequently in consultation with oracles. Names are crucial and it is in this light that Adam's task of naming all the creatures should be understood. To name is to select and focus on an aspect of reality and to control, define, and shape reality. In other words, to name is to create, and by taking part in naming, Adam becomes a partner in creation. Naming the creatures also gives Adam dominion over them. In the same way, God's naming of Adam is a manifestation of his dominion over Adam. When he allows Adam to name Eve, it is clear that woman is considered subordinate.

In the Biblical tradition, a person's name embodies his or her essence. When the essence changes, there is a corresponding change in name. Abram becomes Abraham at the time of his covenant with God, and Sarai becomes Sarah. Jacob, after wrestling with the angel, becomes Israel. Naomi ("sweet"), after the death of her children, becomes Mara ("bitter"). The conflict in the Old Testament between the matriarchal and patriarchal principles in naming emerges when Rachel, dying in childbirth, names her son Benomi (whose meaning is obscure but is believed to be "son of my suffering"). Jacob takes the child from the dying Rachel and renames him Benjamin ("son of my right [hand or side]"), thus going against a deathbed wish and establishing the patriarchal power to name and the priority of "right."

8

Is God Male or Female?

THROUGH AN analysis of matriarchy and patriarchy we have seen how all-pervasive these categories are,
how deeply they affect our perception of reality. We have
shown that a matriarchal or patriarchal religion is more
than a religion in which the central deity is female or male.
It involves our relationship to other beings, how we confront death, how we find meaning, and other important
concerns. In short, the matriarchal or patriarchal character
of our religion determines how we order our values. Matriarchy and patriarchy are two fundamental and opposing
ways of life in this world and of understanding reality.

Up to now we have been content to explore the deep-
rootedness and implications of the concepts of matriarchy
and patriarchy without considering their "status": are they
the products of biology, of socialization, or are they written
into the nature of things? This is the crucial question con-
fronting any serious investigation from the psychological,
educational, or ethical viewpoint. Is what we are and what
we can be written into the genoplasm or can we be free to
choose our own values? The twentieth-century form of
this debate has been taken up by Noam Chomsky in linguistics, Jean Piaget in educational psychology, and Jean-Paul
Sartre in ethics.[1] Briefly, the debate centers on the question

of "a given." Do we come into the world with a predeter- mined essence—a "human nature"—or do we create our- selves by interacting with our environment? Existentialist writers, such as Sartre and Albert Camus, see in this ques- tion the ethical issue of human freedom and hence, human responsibility. If we are to have responsibility for who we are, then we must create ourselves and reject the idea of a "human nature." Neo-Kantians, on the other hand, also see the question as central to ethics but come to the opposite conclusion. In their view, ethics is only meaningful if its judgments are universal, but this is possible only if there is a shared reality—that is, all humans perceive the world in the same way. But a shared reality depends on mankind's having a predetermined essence.

In either case, the question is: Are there innate ideas? The term "innate ideas" itself could refer either to actual content (the idea of the existence of God),[2] to a collective unconscious (memories of the race),[3] or to forms of thought (the way we structure, organize, and arrange thought). It is this last notion of innateness, presented by Kant,[4] that is the subject of the twentieth-century debate and that is rele- vant for this investigation of matriarchy and patriarchy. Chomsky emphatically reaffirms the concept of innateness. He believes that the deep structure of language—the under- lying rules governing its formation and grammar—is in- nate in humans. Further, while experience might be needed to stimulate the use of these ideas, the ideas themselves do not come from experience. People come into the world with these forms of thought as part of their human makeup.

Piaget holds that there are innate forms of thought,

though he explains that the potentiality for these ideas may atrophy if experience does not stimulate it (much as a potentially healthy leg may lose its strength if it is not exercised). Still, the potentiality is innate in all mankind. Piaget's concept of innateness is even more far-reaching than Chomsky's in that it includes the development of moral thought and scientific conceptualization as well as symbol development.[5]

The innateness argument cuts two ways. On the one hand it gives us a shared experience of the world and thereby the ability for universal judgments. It rules out elitism because the difference between two individuals (given the same innate inheritance) depends upon the difference in the opportunities and experiences that they have been allowed to enjoy. On the other hand (and this is what troubles Sartre), it relieves humans of crucial responsibility and moves some of the most important moral concepts out of the domain of judgment. If what people are and how they think is a product of innate categories of the mind, then people are not responsible or free to be other than they are. But Sartre considers freedom, that is, the freedom to define ourselves, to be the very essence of what it is to be human. We define other things by creating them for a purpose: for instance, we create knives to cut and define knives in terms of their cutting function. But human beings are valuable in and of themselves, created to serve no other function and hence as yet undefined. In Sartre's view, humans can be free of all forces acting upon them and can therefore be responsible not only for what they do, but for the thought processes that lead to their actions as well.

The Kantian Revolution

The foregoing brief sketch hardly does justice to the profound thoughts and carefully constructed systems of Chomsky, Piaget, and Sartre. The important point is that implicit in the ideas of Piaget and Chomsky is the notion of universal innate ideas. Because this question is treated more directly and extensively in Kant than by anyone later, it is easiest to examine it within the Kantian formulation. This requires stepping back for a moment in the history of philosophy.

Kant caused a major revolution in thought with his discussion of innate categories of the mind. He put the question in terms of the problems of what can be known, one of the basic philosophical questions since the time of the ancient Greeks. Philosophers generally accepted that knowledge required both an object of knowledge and a subject, or a known and a knower. Yet in trying to answer the question of what can be known, attention was always focused on the object, the thing to be known. In his approach to the problem, Kant chose to examine the subject, or more specifically, what the knower brings to the object to be known. Here, as in other examples we will see below, the insight comes with the reframing of the question. As long as people focused on the object to be known, the issue was limited to the question of knowable qualities versus fleeting characteristics (or, essence versus accident). The only differences of opinion were in identifying what was essential and what accidental.

In a remarkable break with the past, Kant focused on the knower. According to Kant, the knower never comes to reality empty and free, but comes with innate categories of the mind that structure and give meaning to his perceptions. In other words, our minds are not blank tablets on which perceptions are then written. Our minds actively structure reality in terms of an innate "grid." This grid organizes data in terms of space and time, quality, quantity, cause and effect—all of which are not themselves perceptions from the external world but our innate tools for dealing with the world. So the knower in Kant's system never "sees" reality as it is, but "sees" it as organized by the knower's own innate categories of the mind. An example of such a process, according to Kant, is "causality." We can never actually observe a "cause" in nature—we can only observe that event "A" precedes event "B." The concept of causality is one of the categories by which we understand and order our perceptions of reality.

Much of what can be said about Kant's categories is applicable to our categories of matriarchy and patriarchy. They too structure our reality and order our values; they too become the shared conceptual framework and point of reference for judgments in a society; and they too are central in the debate on innateness, for if the conceptual category of matriarchy accompanies the biologically female person as an adjunct to secondary sex characteristics, then biology is indeed destiny and Sartre's freedom is an illusion.

Let us review some of the points of Kant's categories. It was at once the subtlest form of skepticism ever put forth—that is, people can never hope to know reality— and yet a solution to solipsism, that is, we can go beyond pure subjectivity and relativism to meaningful statements and judgments among people. Skepticism is the position that claims that we can never know reality. In its earlier forms, skepticism was based on some flaw in the object to be known (it was always in a process of change, for example). Kant agreed that we could never know reality (the thing in itself) but argued that the obstacle to knowledge is the person. We come with an internal filter that admits some perceptions, rejects others, and orders and evaluates those it does admit. The usual result of skepticism had been a rejection of universal ethical judgments: if no two people can experience the same reality, who could set a standard or make a judgment? Kant overcame that implication of skepticism by asserting that we have a common reality because we all share the same categories of the mind.

The Kantian position was revolutionary on two counts. First, in dealing with the problem of knowledge, the focus was shifted from "what can be known" to the knower—a position that influenced all subsequent thought on the problem. Second, once it is conceded that discussions about time, space, causality, etc., have as their subject matter not reality but the way we structure or think about reality, then the door is opened to the possibility that there may be other ways to construe reality, that is, categories other than those worked out by Kant. This is a crucial point, although it is one that Kant himself did not explore because he concluded that the categories of the mind were universal. But the idea that other categories may exist becomes a live possibility once it is accepted that what we call perceptions come to us imbedded within a conceptual scheme. Since categories are not part of known reality but what the knower brings to reality, then they are of immense importance and the possibility of other categories has the most serious implications for religion and ethics. What is more, how we acquire these categories and transmit them becomes a question fraught with ethical import.

The first chink in the Kantian position was made by a neo-Kantian, Ernst Cassirer. Cassirer showed that Kant's "universal" categories were not always universal. He pointed out, for example, that reason, or scientific thought, is often abandoned under certain conditions in favor of another mode of thought, a mode he described as more primitive. In times of disaster, our highly sophisticated concept of causality often gives way to superstitious modes of causality. We fight the impending disaster with imitative magic or by avoiding anything which through contiguity of time or place has become associated with the disaster.[6] Our thinking is "mythic" and Cassirer recognized the resemblance between our thought under stress and the thought processes of archaic societies.

Freud's work supports Cassirer's findings. Freud showed the loss of symbol development in certain apractic disorders. In other words, the Kantian concepts of causality, time, and space do not come naturally to us. Since mythic thought has different meanings of "cause" and "time," it comes up with a different experience of reality. Cassirer thus challenged Kant on one level and accepted him on another. He felt that the Kantian categories were in fact an achievement over earlier mythic thought and pointed out that some societies had yet to reach the Kantian level and still operated on the "archaic" or mythic level. While Cassirer disagrees, then, on the *absolute* universality of the categories, he does seem to accept the idea of a universality within any society and the innateness of these categories.

These categories, as we saw earlier, function in the same way as the categories of matriarchy and patriarchy. As with matriarchy and patriarchy, they structure reality and value. The crucial question is, Do we have a choice? Are the categories really innate or could they be other than they are? It seems an unnecessary mystification to call these categories "innate." No one is really arguing that an infant taken from a mythic society (and there are mythic societies contemporaneous with rational societies) and raised in our post-Newtonian world would retain the mythic categories of time, space, and causality. The term "innate" is applied here to express that these categories are not deliberately and consciously adopted. In other words, "innate," as it is used here, does not mean something irrevocably transmitted through the genoplasm but rather, it means something unconsciously acquired.

The Kantian categories of space and time have been proven not be be universally held. Mythic societies have a different concept, carefully delineated by Cassirer. These categories do not even hold true for Western European society. The major twentieth-century scientific breakthrough came about as a result of a direct challenge to the Kantian (Newtonian) concept of space and time. If the concepts are genuinely innate and universal, there could have been no Einsteinian breakthrough. If they are not universal, then what is meant by innate? It seems to be the non-deliberate, the unconscious, the unexamined.

If these categories structure our whole perception of
reality and value and are unconsciously acquired, the remaining question is, Can an unconscious process become
conscious? What happens if an unquestioning acceptance is
questioned? Kant took the first step in recognizing that
there were categories. Recognizing that our perception of
reality is mediated by categories of the understanding already puts a different perspective on these categories: they
are now conscious. If we also recognize that these categories
are not universal and could be other, more possibilities open
up. Those experiences that we denied because they did not
make sense within our categories of the understanding once
more claim our attention. What is more, once we recognize
that we can scrutinize, modify, and even choose our conceptual categories, we realize that it is our highest ethical
obligation to do so. If these categories determine our stance
toward the rest of creation, then they are of overriding importance. Sartre has argued that the essence of humanity
is freedom and responsibility. If we are free to choose, then
we are also responsible for the choices we make. When we
recognize that things can be otherwise, we take upon ourselves the responsibility for imperfection and the challenging task to so change our way of thinking that things can
be changed and inequities can be diminished.

When an Unconscious Process Becomes Conscious

This analysis of matriarchy and patriarchy is written on the
optimistic assumption that understanding can make a real
difference. To understand alternative categories is to be free

to make a real choice and it is this choice of conceptual views of reality that allows us to be truly moral beings. Let us return to the fundamental religious questions and see what alternatives have been available within the matriarchal/patriarchal framework. These questions and answers are religious in two different senses and it now becomes important to distinguish between them. The first sense of religion is the traditional institutionalized religion, specifically the Judaeo-Christian tradition. It includes the stories of the Scriptures and the answers for basic human concerns formulated within this tradition. It should be kept in mind that the same institutionalized religious tradition nourished Western secular thought as well and that the concept of "time," for example, in patriarchal science is the same as that in patriarchal religion. The second sense of religion, most clearly expressed in the writings of Paul Tillich,[7] comprises our stance in relation to the rest of creation: our concept of value, our view of death, our fundamental axioms (unexamined principles). In this second sense our choice of matriarchy, patriarchy, or neither is clearly a religious dilemma. It is not only in our institutionalized church but in our confrontation with reality that we must make a commitment.

The Questions

1. One of the first questions addressed in the context of religion concerns the nature of the Deity. Two aspects of this question concern us here: Is God male, female, both, neither, other? and What is our relationship to God? The

second aspect, as we saw earlier, is directly related to the
first. In matriarchy, God is female, and the relationship of
God to people follows the mother-child model. Even though
male gods enter the pantheon (for sex is fundamental to
matriarchy and the female deities need male partners), the
major God is female, creation is material, and concern is
with this world. In patriarchy, God is male and his basic
relationship to the world is judgmental. Creation is rational
and concern is with a perfect realm.

These are the two alternatives we have explored thus far.
A third possibility suggests itself: perhaps the happy solution would be to combine the experiences of matriarchy and
patriarchy and see God as both female and male. This position finds Biblical support in the verse "In the divine image
created he him, male and female created he them."[8] The
text suggests that Eve is no less in the image of God than
Adam is, that is, that God is androgynous. The concept of
an androgynous God has been advanced in mystical writings and appeared in ancient Greece as well. In Greek society the androgyne was a religious ideal. The androgyne
was *not* biologically androgynous (a deformity that usually
warranted exposure in the case of a newborn infant) but
psychologically. Androgyny was frequently equated with
holiness or attributed to a holy person. Johann Wilhelm
Ritter suggests that Christ was androgynous[9] and Georg
Koepgen attributes androgyny not only to Christ, but to the
church and its priests as well.[10] In this connection, Eliade
has suggested that the dress of priests (skirts) served the
purpose of representing their androgynous nature. The concept of an androgynous Deity as the cause of creation is

found in the Kabbalah, in the teachings of alchemy, in the writings of the mystic Jacob Boehme, and in the Gnostic *Gospel of Thomas, Gospel of Philip,* and *Gospel according to the Egyptians.*[11] Midrashic Jewish tradition holds that Adam/Eve was originally an androgynous being, that the fall consisted of the separation of maleness and femaleness, and that we will regain Eden when we become whole again.

As attractive as this position may be, I suggest that it cannot be the final position although it is perhaps a necessary way station. Having lived so long within a patriarchal system, it is essential for us to reclaim and legitimize feminine attributes both for humanity and for the Ground of Being. But a historical necessity should not be made into a metaphysical necessity. We must not freeze the concept of Deity in our own historical set. Right now we have lived with generations of patriarchy and only begun to recognize and reclaim matriarchy but it is certainly conceivable that this duality is not built into the nature of things. God need not be male and female, for what we take to be opposing pairs of concepts may, from a larger perspective, not be in opposition at all. The change in thinking that I suggest is more difficult than a change from "Our father which art in Heaven" to "Our parents which art in Heaven." In other words, the concept of an androgynous God is based on the idea of the *coincidentia oppositorum*—the union of opposites—but if maleness and femaleness are not opposed to begin with, then the concept of an androgynous God may not prove any more successful in meeting the need for a way of understanding the nature of the Deity.

2. The second question logically follows from the first: what
is our concept of meaning and value? As suggested earlier,
our view of the nature of our creator and of the mode of
creation affects our concepts of meaning and value. Another
way of saying this is that what we mean by "God" is our
ground of reality—our way of understanding and evalu-
ating what is. Our cosmology is related to the concept of
meaning we have chosen. If God creates us as does a
mother, our experiences take on meaning in one way. If
God, the artist, creates us to fulfill a function, our experiences take on meaning in another way.

The question of meaning is twofold: What is the meaning of life? and How ought we to live? In matriarchy, life
is considered an intrinsic good and being itself provides
the meaning. As for the problem of how we ought to live,
the solution is related to the cyclical nature of time—what
is, has been. We derive our standard of value from earlier
exemplars, who have been what we now are. What it is to
be a mother, wife, or hero has been defined and we attempt
to live up to the model. In patriarchy the answers are different. Life itself is directed toward an ideal of perfection, an
end of days, a utopian society. Our meaning is achieved by
contributing to this *teleos*. If we accept *neither* matriarchy
nor patriarchy and deny that God created us, then meaning
and value lie vulnerable unless we can find some universal
principle in which to ground them, such as human nature,
the value of life, or the form of the good.

Once again I submit that the choices considered thus far
are not enough. Mother and artist do not really exhaust the
possibilities of creative relationships and even these alterna-

tives can be further explored. We have dealt with how the artist creates the work of art but have not considered the effect of the creation on the creator. In a sense, the act creates the doer even as the doer acts.

This causal relationship needs further scrutiny. Social scientists are lately accepting a view of causality modeled on Newton's third law of motion, which states that "For every action there is an equal and opposite reaction." In other words, if "A" has an effect on "B," then "B" has a reciprocal effect on "A"; there can be no purely one-sided causality. In cosmic terms, this would mean that if God is known through God's effects and humans are among these effects, then what we become determines in part who God is. God is defined through this world—the creation or effects of God's causality. Moreover, since this world is changing, God too changes, both as evidenced by creation and as caused by the creation, for the act of creation changes and transforms the creator. From this perspective the horrible paradox of evil loses its paradoxicality. The existence of evil need not be explained away. Evil exists because we are not yet good and hence God is not yet good. God is both our creator and our creation, our ancestor and our descendent.

This discussion of creation, a form of causality, has been based on an unexamined notion of causality. But we have just brought out the Kantian view that causality is not a fact about reality but a way that the mind understands and organizes perceptions. This concept of creation will be examined further in the last chapter.

3. The problem of evil is the single most difficult problem
facing traditional religion. Why do the good suffer and the
evil seem to thrive? The problem is universal in that everyone has either personally experienced or personally wit-
nessed the seemingly unfair distribution of suffering. How
can a definition of God as good and just be reconciled with
these human experiences? Attempts to dispel the problem
of evil have usually raised as many questions as they had
sought to answer. We are asked to deny the reality of evil,
but if we are misperceiving good as evil, isn't that itself
an evil? We are told that God's ways are not our ways and
we cannot hope to understand them, but what comfort and
moral guidance can an incomprehensible God provide?
Moreover, if God is really the source of our moral code (the
giver of the Ten Commandments), his ways clearly are our
ways. Finally, we are told that all will be righted in the
world to come, but what greater good then could possibly
be served by or compensate for the suffering of the inno-
cent now?

The concept of evil is really composed of two separate
strands. It is important to unravel them, because what
serves as an answer for one may not serve as an answer
for the other. There is evil suffered at the hands of others
(cruelty, injustice) and there is impersonal evil, suffered at
the hand of nature (drought, accident). The traditional concept of God takes both of these aspects into account. To
deal with the first, or "moral" aspect of evil, God is said
to be a just God who can assure the eventual triumph of
justice. But the just God who triumphs over injustice makes

our own struggles against evil meaningless—or moral struggles can be meaningful only if the results are not assured
and our efforts may tip the balance. To deal with human
pain and suffering, or "physical" evil, God is described as
a God who cares and who suffers in and through our suffering. The caring God assures us of nothing but is one
with us in pain. But while sharing the pain may ease it
somewhat, the sharing does not give meaning to the pain
or justify its infliction.

The two attributes of God invoked in the consideration
of evil coincide with the familiar characterizations of God
as just (patriarchal) and compassionate (matriarchal). Unfortunately, neither characterization adequately aids us in
understanding evil nor does combining the two serve us
better.

4. How do we feel about the world? Our evaluation of the
material world is related to the way in which we deal with
the other religious questions. If permanence, eternity, law,
and the God of justice are emphasized, then this material
world is seen as a trap and our ties to this world are evil.
If change, growth, spontaneity, and the God of compassion
are emphasized, then this world is glorified and we feel akin
to all of material creation. The dualistic formulation forces
a choice between meaning in this world and meaning in
another world, homeland and exile, yet choosing either
alternative contradicts felt experience. We do not feel completely at one with creation—our self-consciousness sets
us apart. But we are not totally estranged either—our life

cycles are in harmony with the animals and plants around us. The solution of the *coincidentia oppositorum*, which can be interpreted as accepting both alternatives, still admits of the *existence* of two opposing alternatives. It is this dualistic formulation of the problem that stands in the way of a solution.

5. How do we understand death? The way we view death is related to our feelings about change, creativity, and life. The argument that death and destruction are essential so that we can all be creative is unsatisfactory for someone who values neither creativity nor the wonder and mystery of transformation and growth. For that person, the idea of a changeless world to which death is the entrance is more apt to prove consoling. Once again the either/or formulation is not satisfactory. Even if we accept the need for destruction so that life can be renewed, we wish that we could somehow stand outside the process to understand it and to be untouched by it. There is a yearning for a consciousness that will remain intact while assenting to and witnessing its own destruction. Yet even as we long for another world, there are things about this world that we find infinitely sweet. We long for the very transformations that move us closer to death: the vibrant new life of spring and the brilliant poignancy of autumn. We fear the sterile stasis of perfection and the changeless.

6. How do we understand life? Is it meaningful in and of itself or only as it moves toward some goal—whether that goal be another world or a different state of this world?

Current Choices

Those are the fundamental religious questions as seen
in the perspective of the controversy between matriarchy
and patriarchy. If those opposing formulations are now
better understood than previously, are we still helpless
to do anything but recognize our inevitable and unchanging roles and adjust to them? Or are we in a position to choose matriarchy consciously, reject it entirely, or
try somehow to work out a compromise system encom-
passing both matriarchy and patriarchy? Each of these four
solutions to the controversy has been seriously advanced
by one or more writers in the context of the feminist move-
ment of the nineteen seventies. M. Esther Harding, after
drawing out the archetype of female, sees as the central
problem "how she [woman] may adapt to the masculine
and feminine *principles* which rule her from within."[12] In
other words woman (and man) is not free in the Sartrian
sense, but free only to recognize the forces which rule her.
Understanding the archetype still leaves her destined to her
role. Harding claims that "These laws or principles [mas-
culine and feminine] are inherent in the nature of things
and function unerringly and inevitably."[13] Woman's health
and psychological well-being depend upon her fostering of
the feminine principle within herself. "Not infrequently we
hear it affirmed that there is no essential difference between
men and women, except the biological one. Many women
have accepted this standpoint and have themselves done
much to foster it. They have been content to be men in
petticoats and so have lost touch with the feminine prin-

ciple within themselves."[14] Harding's view is deterministic
and assigns to each person—according to gender—his or
her station and its duties.

Elizabeth Gould Davis argues for the primacy and supremacy of women. This position is based on the idea that
"In the beginning there was woman," where the male is
denied a role in creation just as the female is denied it in
patriarchy. Davis claims that patriarchy has relegated
women to a subordinate role but that in time ". . . woman
will again predominate. She who was revered and wor-
shiped by early man because of her power to see the unseen
will once again be the pivot—not as sex but as divine
woman—about whom the next civilization will, as of old,
revolve."[15] This idea is somewhat reminiscent of the senti-
ment expressed by the nineteenth-century song writer
and abolitionist Henry Clay Work: "We will be the massa's,
they will be the slaves."[16] Underlying this line of reasoning
is the belief that one group must always predominate and
subjugate the other.

Midge Decter accepts the view that women are naturally
inferior. "To insist that women have been twisted into the
shapes of inferiority by a power beyond their control is
still to offer one's assent to the idea that they are inferior."[17] She argues that the fact that women have not, up
to now, disputed male sovereignty is proof that there is
nothing wrong with the status quo. The fact that women
now dispute male sovereignty proves that there is something wrong not with the status quo but with contemporary
women.

Carolyn Heilbrun has avoided the inevitability of Hard-

ing. She feels that an understanding of the concepts of
feminine and masculine can lessen the polarity. She has
also avoided the one-sidedness of Davis. While she tends
to emphasize the feminine concepts, she does so in an effort
to compensate for the high esteem in which the masculine
traits are held in the Western tradition. She favors a true
reconciliation of the sexes in androgyny, a concept which
sees a full human being as having the traits of both male
and female. Androgyny is a major step forward in that it
restores women to a major position in the Godhead without
alienating men (as matriarchy might). The position of androgyny is put forward with humane motivations. It is a
clear position of combining our conflicting experiences.[18]

In urging a union of the feminine and the masculine,
androgyny shares the matriarchal and patriarchal assumption that the distinction between the two is real. To say that
"In Christ there is neither male nor female . . ." is to affirm
the distinction even as you deny its application. To con-
ceive of God as androgynous is to admit of a basic contradiction which is resolved in God. But it is this very
contradiction, which has served also as a basic assumption
of matriarchy and patriarchy, that can now be challenged.
If the categories of masculine and feminine can be redefined
so that they are no longer in opposition, it should be possible to go beyond androgyny to a world view that does
not carry within it the seeds of its own destruction.

9

A New Perspective

HAVING REJECTED the solutions we saw earlier, I must now find a new alternative. I suggested earlier that major breakthroughs occurred in philosophy when a philosopher refused to accept the assumptions implicit in the formulation of the question. We saw this with the Kantian revolution. Three additional examples demonstrate this point. The first involves the assumed irreconcilable opposition of knowledge and change.

The early Greek philosophers believed there could be no knowledge of that which changes—that there was an irreconcilable duality between knowledge and change. If knowledge could exist, then change must be an illusion. This is what Zeno's paradoxes sought to demonstrate in proving that motion was impossible. If, on the other hand, change existed, then there could be no hope of real knowledge, hence all was relative, and man was the measure of all things. And so the sides lined up in the Greek world.

Heraclitus believed that change was a real fact about the world, so knowledge was impossible. Parmenides felt that knowledge was a reality so change must be an illusion. Plato maintained that there could only be knowledge of the changeless and that this world, which is a world of change, could not itself be known. But he postulated the changeless

forms which he considered the true subject matter of
knowledge. It was Aristotle who refused to accept the
formulation of the question and the assumption that knowledge and change were irreconcilable opposites. He held that
the process of change itself could be the subject matter of
knowledge. He did not accept the earlier solutions of the
presence of change with the absence of knowledge or the
presence of knowledge with the absence of change, or even
the presence of change and the presence of the knowable
in Plato's formulation. He rejected the duality and discovered a new subject matter for knowledge. In other words,
by refusing to accept a duality—an irreconcilable opposition between knowledge and change—Aristotle put a
whole new perspective on the problem of knowledge.

Another problem based on a supposed irreconcilable
duality is the mind-body problem. Mind and body were
understood to be two radically different substances that
existed apart from each other. Being categorically separate
and opposed components of reality, they could have no
attributes in common and their interaction was a theoretical
impossibility. The range of solutions offered to the mind-
body problem included the following: (1) the *supposed* interaction is just a supposition because in reality there is no
body—all is spirit and body is an illusion; (2) the "interaction" is possible because mind is illusory and the only
reality is matter and motion; (3) mind exists and body
exists and they interact but *how* this occurs is an insoluble
dilemma, a theological mystery; (4) God causes the body
to act when the mind wills it to act; (5) mind and body by
some mysterious force are joined in the pineal gland (this

tells where but not how); and (6) mind and body do not interact in a causal sense but by a pre-existent harmony: when it is time for the body to be stuck by a pin, it is time for the mind to feel pain. Once again, the "breakthrough" involved denying the way the problem had been formulated. Spinoza, in answer to the Cartesian mind-body problem, began by asserting that there is no opposition between mind and body. Mind and body are two different ways of construing the same single, monistic reality.

Monism, the view being described here, is the belief in the fundamental oneness or unity of Reality. Reality may be known in many different ways but in fact there is only one underlying Reality. Just as the graph of $X^2 + Y^2 = 9$ is not in opposition to the equation, so the mind is not in opposition to the body, but rather the mind is the idea of the body. Interaction is no longer a problem because there aren't two things: there is one thing understood in two different ways. As did Aristotle before him, Spinoza denied the premise that had left the problem insoluble for so long and redefined the relationship between the underlying categories, mind and body. To say that the mind is the idea of the body—that they are not in opposition to one another but actually one reality expressed in different ways—is to reject the fundamental categories.

In the twentieth century, rejection of another dichotomy was involved with a scientific breakthrough. Since classical thought, a distinction had been drawn between that which imparts motion (energy) and that which is moved (matter). Aristotle, in fact, called the soul *anima*, because it animates or gives motion to the otherwise inert body. The distinction

between matter and energy was retained in Newtonian
physics. Einstein rejected the distinction and showed that
matter and energy were two aspects of the same reality.
Another victim of the Einsteinian revolution was Kant's
dichotomy between space and time.

What Einstein did with regard to matter and energy,
Spinoza with mind and body, and Aristotle with knowledge
and change, is precisely what I feel must be done with the
apparent opposition of matriarchy and patriarchy. I reject
dualism, be it the duality of knowledge and change, mind
and body, or matriarchy and patriarchy. While method-
ologically we may define things in opposition, we know
that what truly is other cannot be part of a shared reality.

An anonymous kabbalist hinted at a similar position,
which is summarized as follows:

> The Torah [five books of Moses] manifests itself under
> two aspects: that of the "Tree of Life" and that of the
> "Tree of the Knowledge of Good and Evil." The latter
> aspect is characteristic of the period of exile. As the Tree
> of Knowledge comprises good *and* evil, so that Torah
> deriving from it comprises permission and prohibition,
> pure and impure; in other words, it is the law of the
> Bible and of rabbinic tradition. In the age of redemption,
> however, the Torah will manifest itself under the aspect
> of the Tree of Life, and all previous distinctions will pass
> away. . . . The pure essence of the Torah will be revealed
> and its outer shell cast off.[1]

The mystic author of these intriguing ideas holds that
our period of exile, since the expulsion from Eden, is characterized by the Tree of Knowledge of Good and Evil, that

is, by the distinctions between permission and prohibition, pure and impure—in other words, dualism. Perhaps, at first glance, his position seems like a sort of androgyny, or *coincidentia oppositorum*. But he does not believe that both the Tree of Life and the Tree of Knowledge of Good and Evil will be restored. The concept of duality, or bifurcation, and subsequent completeness achieved through a union of opposites is gone—because opposition is gone. "All previous distinctions will pass away"—the irreconcilable duality is eliminated and with it the previous insoluble problem.

As this discussion suggests, dualism presents certain problems in understanding Biblical thought. In Paradise there was no dualism. Eden is unity and the Edenic state is at one with the natural world. The promised dominion over nature (and hence opposition to nature) does not occur until the expulsion from the Garden. Genesis 2:10 reads: "A river rises in Eden to water the Garden; outside it forms four separate branch streams." What this pseudo-geographical description symbolizes is that the river is one in Paradise and breaks into multiplicity only outside of Eden. Not only Jewish mystics,[2] but gnostics and structuralists as well,[3] teach that unity is the condition in Paradise and is the underlying belief behind the concept of return, that is, a return from estrangement to oneness.

Once out of Eden, duality appears as pairs of opposites: Cain and Abel, Ishmael and Isaac, Esau and Jacob, Joseph and his brothers, Egypt and Israel. In the Bible, duality is not overcome by reductionism, that is, the destruction of one of the pairs of opposites. For example, good is not achieved by destroying the evil one: Cain is not destroyed but is reconciled; Ishmael, sent off into the desert to perish, is instead sustained because he too has a role to play. Nor is the *nature* of the opposite transformed or subordinated.

In a monistic system there are no dualities. For example, the invisible and visible are one: the unseen world of value, or the holy, is also this world. Also, what Kant termed the "noumenal" and the "phenomenal" are one. Kant held that we could not know an object as it is in itself (the noumenal) but only as it appears to us filtered by our categories of perception (the phenomenal). As we saw earlier, this was a profound insight and made us aware of the boundary conditions of our knowledge. While on an epistemological level (how we come to know things) I accept Kant's analysis, as a monist, I am committed to overcoming this radical skepticism. So although we can indeed make useful distinctions by defining things in opposition, we must also realize that things that are totally other cannot be part of a shared world.

As a monist, then, I believe in the unity of all things: that reality is one, undivided, with no unrelated aspects. What are the real implications of such a position? To examine that, we return to the six religious questions raised earlier. The following discussion of these questions should not be considered a thorough, well-developed philosophical system. Rather, it is a schematized, tentative pointing out of the sort of answer that might be worked out in monism. Nor is it a working out of all the possibilities within monism itself because there are different sorts of monism. For example, monism can be either theistic or atheistic. Or, monism can result from reductionism, that is, the acceptance of one half of a duality, for example, mind *or* matter, idealism *or* materialism. I have rejected reductionism because I believe that it is based on a false dichotomy. I do not believe that the world divides up into matter and spirit, each complete within its own domain. I have chosen to map out a position of theistic monism. My answers represent an attempt to offer a new alternative, but it is offered with an awareness of its sketchy nature, my concern being more to raise questions than to give finished answers.

The Nature of the Deity

The relationship of God to this world has always been defined in terms of opposition: God is spiritual, this world is material; God is transcendent, this world is immanent; God is perfect, this world is imperfect; God is infinite, this world is finite. Grave theological difficulties arise when one tries to account for the relationship of something wholly other with this world: How can a spiritual God create a material world? If God is transcendent, in what way does God's presence or concern come into this world? If God is perfect, why is this world flawed? What constitutes the limit on an infinite God's creation? Theologians, confronted with these problems, have nonetheless retained the doctrine of the otherness of God, frequently at a high theoretical cost. Behind these multiplying dualities is the fundamental duality of creator and creature. If we were to reject this formulation, then the conflicts between spiritual and material, transcendent and immanent, perfect and imperfect, and infinite and finite would also be overcome.

My position is that God is not apart from, separate from, or other than this reality. We, all together, are part of the whole, the All in All. God is not father, nor mother, nor even parents, because God is not other than, distinct from, or opposed to creation.

Spiritual vs. material. If the world is part of what we mean by "God," then God does not end where matter begins. Matter is not opposed to spirit. Matter and spirit are two ways of describing the single reality, God. Matter and spirit are distinguished on an epistemological level (how we come to know things), but not on an ontological level (how things really are). The language of matter, energy, and force is one way of describing reality. The language of symbol, meaning, and value is another way of describing reality. But behind our many languages is one single underlying reality.

Transcendent vs. immanent. God is in the world but is more than the world. I do not hold that God is reduced to the natural world but rather that the natural world is divine. God is in the world but is not the world. God is the place of the world.

Perfect vs. imperfect. Since God contains the world, then this world is perfect, or complete. Reality is equated with perfection. This position has important implications for the problem of evil and will be treated more fully below.

Infinite vs. finite. Finally, this world, with all its relationships, is infinite. The finite points to and participates in the infinite.

Rejection of the creator/creature duality leads to rejection of other dualities as well. The implications of our stance vis-à-vis the rest of creation are enormous. We recognize our interdependence, our part in a larger whole, and the significance of all. What does this really mean? Does it mean that chairs and tables and bookends are God? No. Approaching the question from the opposite end, it means that God is infinite, that there is no limit to God. We cannot say God is everywhere but stops short of our everyday world. Traditional theology has always paid lip service to the infinity of God but carefully excluded the Deity from the world (except for occasional miracles). God was designated as pure spirit and the world as base matter. The theological problems caused by this dualism were great (How can pure spirit be the efficient cause of a material world?) and unnecessary, if we consider that matter and spirit are two aspects of the same reality, God.

But holding that God is not limited and extends to include our material world does not explain our relationship to God. An analogy might be drawn between our relationship to God and the relationship of a cell in your body to yourself. The cell is alive, with an identity of its own. From the perspective of the cell and its fellow cells, it is a whole, not a part. The cell does not "understand" how all the other cells interrelate to form a large entity. Nor does it understand the controlling force of the body of which it is a part and with which it must harmonize its goals. From the cell's perspective, it is a single, atomic individual. From your perspective, the cell is part of what it is to be you, yet you would scarcely expect it to be identified as being you. Its well-being contributes to your general well-being, but is of more concern to itself than to you. A scientist who separated out all the cells in your body still would not have

"you," because you are more than the sum of your cells.
You are the organizing principle that gives pattern and interconnectedness to the cells. The cell lives out its life span
contributing to the whole without ever being aware of the
larger pattern or purpose.

We stand in relation to God as the cell stands in relation
to your body. We too tend to think of ourselves as isolated
individuals, unaware of the essential interrelationship of the
parts to this larger whole. And we can, in fact, live out our
lives without once becoming aware of our place in this
whole. But, unlike the cell, we have the possibility of becoming conscious—not only of our existence—but also of
our role in the system. Through this awareness our lives
can take on new shape and meaning.

Again, it must be emphasized that this is only one conclusion that can be drawn from the rejection of dualism. My
position presupposes an ordering principle, the rejection of
which would change the conclusion in an important way.
The concept of "ordering principle" is used here synony-
mously with "God." That is not to say that God orders the
world (an impossible assumption for monism) but that the
world is ordered. This view shares with science the assumption that there are reasons and that the way we think is not
too different from the way reality is structured; in other
words, understanding is possible.

The Question of Meaning

The rejection of dualism has important implications for the
question of meaning as well. I have dealt in an earlier chap-

ter with the question of meaning in terms of a society's conception of time. If time is considered to be cyclical, meaning for the individual comes through exemplifying a perfect form or archetype. If time is held to be linear, meaning for the individual comes through contributing to some final goal. With the rejection of dualism comes a rejection of the conflict between this world and the world to come—our time here and eternity. Eternity is neither timelessness nor endless temporality, in fact it is not a category of time at all. Eternity is the perspective we can bring to any event when we view it in terms of its relationship to the whole, God. Things are finite when viewed from one perspective and eternal when viewed in their interdependence and contributiveness.

Returning to the question of life and its meaning, life can be said to have value in and of itself—being itself is a good. But life can also be understood in terms of the larger whole toward which we contribute. This world is valuable, but meaning cannot be exhausted by this world. Just as God is infinitely present, so too does God infinitely transcend this realm. What this means in terms of our experience in this world is that we must try to live as fully as possible, finding meaning and value in our own being and uniqueness. From time to time we sense the larger pattern, the interconnectedness, and this infuses our experience with greater depth and dimension. We must understand that there is no meaning "above" our experiences here that challenges or negates our felt meaning. Our sense of meaning is genuine and not in any way diminished by the concept of God or the reality of transcendence.

The Problem of Evil

Evil has two distinct meanings. In one sense of the concept,
evil is measured against an absolute standard: the Objective
Observer judges that action X is unambiguously evil. As a
theistic monist, I cannot accept this meaning of evil because
it rests on two assumptions which I categorically reject.
The first assumption is that there is some external observer
who can make such a judgment. Such an observer would
have to be other than what is observed. But that would con-
tradict our characterization of a monistic God. Moreover,
the notion of an observation point outside the system is incompatible with our view of reality. Finally, I hold that the
observer can never be separated from the observed because
the process of observing itself entails a relationship. The
second assumption is that there is some goal or objective
toward which reality as a whole is moving and that action
X is evil in that it is thwarting this goal. But such a goal
would be external to the world and monism rules out any
external events. This world, right here and now, is, and is
complete.

   In the other sense of the concept, evil is measured against
some identifiable standard: relative to the standard, action
X is evil. This sense of evil is clear, non-mysterious, and
intelligible. Whatever impinges upon us is evil; or, whatever
hinders our desire to persevere in our own being, is evil.
This position allows for two seemingly contradictory views.
It lets us affirm, as I did above, that reality is perfect, and
still lets us find the human situation in need of our efforts
and concern. One of the fullest accounts of the problem of

evil in the second sense of the term is given by Josiah
Royce. Royce evaluates all of the traditional answers to the
problem of Job. He concludes that given Job's assumptions,
there can be no satisfactory answer to the problem of evil;
that as long as God is conceived of as being "out there,"
whether as spectator or as objective observer, no solution is
possible.[4] But if we are a part of what it is to be God, then
we are part of a dynamic process. No one is "doing this to
us"; we accept struggle, tension, and the constant thwarting
of evil in order to grow, change, overcome, and strive
toward some personal notion of perfection. The problem of
evil is very complex and must be dealt with on many different levels. But part of the problem consists in the idea that
someone has meted out this suffering, or at least observed
it and has chosen not to intervene. It is the idea of a God
who tests, judges, or disengages himself that adds to the
confusion and pain of evil. Once this concept of "the other"
is removed, part of the difficulty of the problem is eased.

There is another important aspect of the problem of evil.
When evil is seen as the opposite of good, we can deal with
it only by exclusion, that is, by separating out the evildoer
from the rest of society. When, however, we recognize that
evil and good are part of the same reality we do not see
evildoers as persons totally other than ourselves. We recognize aspects of evildoers in ourselves and thus can deal with
them on the basis of a commonality.

Nevertheless, the problem of evil persists. What good
does it do one to be told that the world is perfect if we experience suffering? Our perceptions must be right, we do
experience suffering. It would be a trivializing of our very
real experience of evil to deny its reality—and it would be

a misinterpretation of monism as well. What we do, experience, and suffer here is real. Monists are not illusionists; they cannot make this world of pain disappear. They can only affirm that our experiences are meaningful—are part of a complete and ordered whole. Monism can also change the perspective: since the suffering is human suffering and the evil is human evil, the solutions must be worked out by people for their needs. I share with existentialists the belief in human freedom and responsibility—but I differ from them in their view of the absurdity of life. Evil is real but not absolute. My final affirmation is one of meaning and value.

Our Relationship to the Material World

In traditional Western thought, our relationship to the material world has been based on a false dichotomy between matter and spirit, matter being corrupt (or at least corruptible) and spirit being pure and unchanging. The problems that arise from denigrating the material world have been drawn out earlier: rejection of material creation and sexuality, denial of transformation mysteries, and finally, denial of this life and this world. We are cut off from our own experiences, strangers to our own bodies, and alienated from the world that supports us. If dualism is denied, however, then the material world and the spiritual world are recognized as two aspects of the same reality and our place in this world is transformed. We are not estranged from our own bodies and their transformation processes. We recognize, with understanding and equanimity, that aging and decay are aspects of growth.

Death

One of the most serious drawbacks of the dualistic position
is that it cuts us off from one half of experience. That which
is totally other cannot be part of, or related to, the rest of
our reality. Regarding death as totally other than life is
making it alien and frightening. Death cannot be incor-
porated into our experience of life. And yet, it is perhaps
because we die and because we are aware of our impending
death that we are truly human and live the sorts of lives
that we do. Elisabeth Kübler-Ross and other writers on
thanatology and death therapy suggest that when the living
can talk about death, acknowledge it, and accept it as a
reality, their lives (even in the case of terminal patients
with limited futures) take on deeper meaning and death itself becomes meaningful.[5]

One of the important ways in which we differ from the
other species is that we are aware of our mortality and this
awareness colors much of our life. Sartre regards death as
the one principle that removes all meaning from life. I not
only disagree, I hold that it is death, and more especially,
our consciousness of death, that allows us to be fully
human, forces us to define ourselves, and allows for the
possibility of meaning. Let me offer an analogy: one painting is not greater than another by virtue of being on a
larger canvas. The greatness of a painting rests upon its
transcending the limitations of the canvas so that the finished work points to the limitless. It achieves this through
form, color, texture, and an interrelationship among the
parts of the painting. In fact, an infinite canvas could not

hold a meaningful painting at all. That is because the meaning of the painting requires the balance of part to whole,
the motion of the eye caused by the interrelated shapes,
and the suggestion of the limitless within the limited, none
of which are possible on an unlimited canvas. I suggest that
the same holds true for human life. What makes us human
and allows for our meaning are the choices we make and
the opportunities we deny ourselves when we choose between alternatives. We choose this and not that and thereby
give value and meaning to life. We do not need an infinite
canvas but one painted with all the creativity we can offer,
so that our substance will be too great to be contained in its
finite form, not too sparse to fill it. This is in part what I
mean by the eternal not being a negation of the temporal
but a different perspective of the same reality.

Life

The monistic view of life is consistent with the view of the
material world described above and our own view of meaning. Life is valuable in itself and in what it points to. It is a
commitment to the process of growth and change, the
thwarting of evil, the acceptance of death.

*   *   *   *   *   *

What I am suggesting is a major revolution. The revolution in knowledge that came about by challenging the
opposition of knowledge and change, mind and body, matter and energy, will be joined by challenging the opposition
of matriarchy and patriarchy. With this challenge will come
the collapse of the opposition inherent in dualism.

NOTES

N.B. Biblical passages from Genesis, Job, Psalms, and John follow the *Anchor Bible* translation. Passages from books that are not yet available in the *Anchor Bible* translation are rendered according to the Revised Standard Version in the *New Oxford Annotated Bible*.

Prologue. In the Beginning

1. For pertinent works of these writers, see Bibliography.

Chapter One. The Frankenstein Motif

1. Freud, *Future of an Illusion*, pp. 18–19.
2. See, for example, Plotinus, *Enneads*, V.1.
3. Job 40:15.
4. Job 42:5.
5. Patai, *Hebrew Goddess*, passim.
6. Genesis 1:27.
7. For example, Genesis 22:1–10 (Isaac); Exodus 1:22 (Hebrews' newborn sons); Exodus 11:4–5 (first-born Egyptians); Judges 11:30–40 (Jephthah's daughter); and 1 Kings 16:34 (sons of Hiel).
8. For example, the expulsion from Eden; the banishment of Cain; the Flood; and the destruction of Sodom and Gomorrah.

9. Goethe, *Faust*, vol. 2, p. 100.
10. For a good discussion of *golem*, see Scholem, "Golem."
11. Concerning the reading, see Bible, *Psalms*, vol. 3, p. 295.
12. Shelley, *Frankenstein*, p. 140.
13. Ibid., p. 33; ibid., p. 52.
14 Genesis 8:21.
15. For example, the heresies of Cerinthus, who proclaimed that Jesus had a natural birth, and Marcion, who proclaimed that Jesus had no earthly parents and that he descended from heaven at the time of his appearance in the synagogue of Capernaum during the fifteenth year of the reign of Tiberius.
16. Erigena, *Periphyseon*, p. 16.

Chapter Two. The Eleusinian Mysteries

1. Mylonas, *Eleusis*, pp. 1–8.
2. Ibid., p. 186.
3. Freud, *Pleasure Principle*, pp. 44–61.
4. Akoun, "Conversation," p. 74.
5. Leach, "Genesis as Myth," p. 10.
6. Freud, "Three Caskets," pp. 293–296.
7. The similarity in the rituals is noted in Neumann, *Great Mother*, p. 312.
8. But note John 12:24: "Unless the grain of wheat falls to the earth and dies, it remains just a grain of wheat. But if it dies, it bears much fruit."
9. Chesterton, *Orthodoxy*, pp. 146–147.
10. Matthew 20:1–16; Luke 15:3–32.
11. Dodds, *Greeks and the Irrational*, p. 75.

Chapter Three. The Sacrifice of Isaac

1. Genesis 22:1–3, 9–13.
2. Graves and Patai, *Hebrew Myths,* p. 174.
3. Spiegel, *Last Trial,* passim.
4. Shalom Spiegel in Ginzberg, *Legends of the Bible,* pp. xxv–xxvi.
5. Ginzberg, *Legends of the Bible,* pp. 127–128.
6. Bakan, *Disease, Pain, and Sacrifice,* pp. 105–110.
7. Genesis 16:2.
8. Genesis 21:7.
9. Genesis 23:1–2.
10. Aeschylus, *Agamemnon,* 1343–1447, in *Oresteia,* pp. 78–82.
11. Ginzberg, *Legends of the Bible,* p. 136.
12. 2 Kings 16:3, 21:6.
13. Judges 11:30–40.
14. 1 Samuel 14:43–45.
15. Micah 6:6–8; Jeremiah 7:30–31, 19:4–6; Ezekiel 16:20–22.
16. Frazer, *New Golden Bough,* pp. 285–303.
17. Soloveitchik, *Lonely Man of Faith,* p. 26.
18. Genesis 25:2, 8–10.
19. Genesis 21:14–20.
20. Kierkegaard, *Fear and Trembling,* p. 122.
21. Genesis 18:25.
22. Genesis 18:19.
23. Sartre, *Existentialism,* pp. 22–23.
24. Heschel, *Passion for Truth,* p. 227.
25. Ibid., p. 49.
26. Bakan, *Duality of Human Existence,* pp. 202–203.
27. Ibid., p. 26.
28. Genesis 12:10–20; 20:1–18.
29. Rashi, commentary on Genesis 25:19 in Bible, *Pentateuch,* pp. 235–239.

30. Romans 9:7.
31. Genesis 18:1–15.
32. Bible, *Genesis*, p. 130.
33. Bakan, *Disease, Pain, and Sacrifice*, p. 119.
34. Talmud, *Baba Bathra*, p. 76–77.
35. Ibid., p. 76–82.
36. Bakan, *Disease, Pain, and Sacrifice*, p. 106.
37. Ginzberg, *Legends of the Jews*, vol. 1, p. 203.
38. Ibid.
39. Ibid., p. 287.

Chapter Four. Wandering

1. Neumann, *Great Mother*, pp. 55–63.
2. Briffault, *The Mothers*, vol. 2, p. 444.
3. Genesis 20:18.
4. Genesis 4:8–9.
5. Bible, *Genesis*, p. 29n.
6. Hooke, *Middle Eastern Mythology*, p. 124.
7. Genesis 4:11.
8. Genesis 11:1–9.
9. Genesis 12:1.
10. Tillich, *On the Boundary*, p. 91.
11. Weil, *Waiting for God*, p. 54.
12. Bachofen, *Myth*, p. 192.
13. 1 Kings 16:29–18:46.
14. Patai, *Hebrew Goddess*, p. 124.
15. These remarks are suggested by Circlot, *Dictionary of Symbols*, p. 76.

Chapter Five. The Feminization of Judaism in the Zohar

1. Scholem, *Major Trends*, p. 156–204.
2. J. Abelson, in *The Zohar*, vol. 1, p. xxiv.
3. Cited ibid., p. xiii–xiv.
4. Cited ibid., p. xviii.
5. This formulation suggested by Maurice Simon in *The Zohar*, vol. 5, pp. 402–405.
6. Maurice Simon in *The Zohar*, vol. 5, p. 403.
7. Zohar 1:2b in *The Zohar*, vol. 1, p. 10 (Romanization regularized).
8. Plato, *Symposium* 190–192.
9. Cohen, *Days of Simon Stern*, p. 279.
10. Maurice Simon in *The Zohar*, vol. 5, p. 396.
11. For a discussion of God as Matronit, see Patai, *Hebrew Goddess*, pp. 186–206.
12. Pines, *Brain Changers*, pp. 138–159.
13. Genesis 22:4.
14. Genesis 22:7.
15. Genesis 22:11.

Chapter Six. The Cult of Mary

1. For example, in Egyptian mythology, the sky goddess Nut gives birth to Isis and Osiris (Hooke, *Middle Eastern Mythology*, p. 72).
2. For example, in Greek mythology, Gaea, mother of Uranos, procreates with him the race of Titans (Diner, *Mothers and Amazons*, p. 2).
3. For example, in Greek mythology, Cybele and Attis; Diana and Virbius; and Aphrodite and Phaethon (Diner, *Mothers and Amazons*, p. 3).

4. Kerényi, *Eleusis*, p. 117; but see Nilsson, *History*, pp. 104, 123, and 212.
5. Harding, *Woman's Mysteries*, p. 147.
6. Neumann, *Great Mother*, pp. 281–305.
7. For a discussion of the triune nature of the goddess, see Graves, *White Goddess*, pp. 383–408, and Harding, *Woman's Mysteries*, pp. 254–256.
8. Neumann, *Great Mother*, pp. 309–311.
9. Hooke, *Middle Eastern Mythology*, pp. 18–65, 79–95, passim, and Patai, *Hebrew Goddess*, pp. 15–52, passim.
10. For example, the Babylonian Epic of Creation contains references to the goddess Tiamat (Hooke, *Middle Eastern Mythology*, p. 44).
11. Patai, *Hebrew Goddess*, pp. 15–17 and 270–274.
12. For example, Jeremiah 44:24–29.
13. Mayor, "Mary," p. 287.
14. Ibid.
15. Mark 3:33, 35.
16. Luke 11:27–28.
17. Mayor, "Mary," p. 287.
18. Patai, *Hebrew Goddess*, p. 273.
19. Mechtild, *Revelations*, p. 13.
20. See, for example, Diner, *Mothers and Amazons*, p. 4.
21. Matthew 27:55–56.
22. Neumann, *Great Mother*, plates 47, 94, 95.
23. Wycliffe, quoted in Mayor, "Mary," p. 287.
24. Hrotswitha of Gandersham, quoted in Heiler, "Madonna," p. 361.
25. Goethe, *Faust*, vol. 2, p. 288.
26. Mayor, "Mary," p. 292.
27. Ibid.
28. Neumann, *Great Mother*, pp. 39–54.

29. Heiler, "Madonna," p. 356.
30. Reproduced in Neumann, *Great Mother*, plates 176–177.
31. Graves, *White Goddess*, p. 142.
32. Kerényi, "Mysteries," pp. 55–56.
33. Gressmann, "Tod und Auferstehung," p. 24.
34. Heiler, "Madonna," p. 373.

Chapter Seven. Characteristics of Matriarchal Religions

1. Campbell, *Masks of God: Primitive*, p. 23.
2. Harding, *Woman's Mysteries*, p. 64.
3. Bachofen, *Myth*, p. 77.
4. Patai, *Hebrew Goddess*, p. 52.
5. Hooke, *Middle Eastern Mythology*, p. 93.
6. Deuteronomy 12:29–31.
7. Hooke, *Middle Eastern Mythology*, p. 24.
8. Graves and Patai, *Hebrew Myths*, p. 23.
9. Hooke, *Middle Eastern Mythology*, p. 71.
10. Diner, *Mothers and Amazons*, p. 2.
11. Aristotle, *Metaphysics*, 1028a31–1028b2.
12. Hooke, *Middle Eastern Mythology*, p. 24.
13. Bible, *Genesis*, p. 44, inexplicably omits translation of the Hebrew words *ve-yaldu lahem*.
14. Harrelson, *Fertility Cult*, p. 54.
15. Graves and Patai, *Hebrew Myths*, p. 26.
16. Ibid., p. 31.
17. Bachofen, *Myth*, p. 132.
18. Ibid., p. 155.
19. Plato, *Phaedo*, 66b–67b.
20. Kant, *Critique*, p. 74.

21. Cassirer, *Symbolic Forms*, vol. 2, pp. 104–118; Eliade, *Myth of Eternal Return*, pp. 34–48.
22. Freud, *Moses and Monotheism*, pp. 10–14; Rank, *Birth of Hero*, pp. 3–13; Eliade, *Myth of Eternal Return*, pp. 46–48.
23. Worringer, *Abstraction and Empathy*, pp. 20–25.
24. Diner, *Mothers and Amazons*, p. 50.
25. Zohar 1:5b in *The Zohar*, vol. 1, p. 22.
26. Diner, *Mothers and Amazons*, pp. 45–46.
27. Straus, "Upright Posture," p. 535.
28. Sophocles, *Oedipus at Colonus*, 1584–85.
29. Salk, "Role of the Heartbeat."
30. Pines, *Brain Changers*, pp. 138–159.
31. Cirlot, *Dictionary of Symbols*, p. 58.
32. Bachofen, *Myth*, p. 121.

Chapter Eight. Is God Male or Female?

1. Chomsky, *Cartesian Linguistics*; Piaget, *Genetic Epistemology*; Sartre, *Being and Nothingness*.
2. As in Meditation III in Descartes, *Meditations*, pp. 157–171.
3. As in Jung, "Concept," pp. 59–60.
4. Kant, *Critique*, pp. 104–119.
5. Piaget, *Moral Judgment*, pp. 7–9, 197–325.
6. Cassirer, *Symbolic Forms*, vol. 2, pp. 60–70.
7. Tillich, *Dynamics of Faith*, pp. 1–29.
8. Genesis 1:27.
9. Eliade, *Two and the One*, p. 101.
10. Koepgen, *Gnosis*, pp. 316 ff.
11. Eliade, *Two and the One*, pp. 103–107.
12. Harding, *Woman's Mysteries*, p. 12.

13. Ibid., p. 16.
14. Ibid., p. 17.
15 Davis, *First Sex*, p. 339.
16. From the song *Babylon Is Fallen*.
17. Decter, *New Chastity*, p. 41.
18. Heilbrun, *Androgyny*, pp. ix–xxi.

Chapter Nine. A New Perspective
1. Scholem, *Sabbatai Sevi*, pp. 11–12.
2. Scholem, *Kabbalah and Its Symbolism*, p. 69.
3. Pallis, "Problem of Evil," passim; Leach, "Lévi-Strauss in Eden," chart, p. 392.
4. Royce, "Problem of Job."
5. Kübler-Ross, *On Death and Dying*, pp. 112–137.

BIBLIOGRAPHY

N.B. Reprints are listed chiefly for older works.

Aeschylus.
Oresteia. Translated by Richmond Lattimore. Chicago: University of Chicago Press, 1953.

Akoun, André, Françoise Morin, and Jacques Mousseau.
"The Father of Structural Anthropology Takes a Misanthropic View of Lawless Humanism: A Conversation with Claude Lévi-Strauss," translated by Anthony Wilden, in *Psychology Today*, vol. 5, no. 12 (May 1972), pp. 36–39, 74–82. [Originally published in French.]

Albright, William Foxwell.
From the Stone Age to Christianity: Monotheism and the Historical Process. 2nd ed. with a new introduction. Garden City, N.Y.: Doubleday, 1957. [1st ed. 1940.]

Aristotle.
Metaphysics. Translated by W. D. Ross. In *The Basic Works of Aristotle*. Edited by Richard McKeon. New York: Random House, 1941. Pp. 681–9266.

Bachofen, Johann Jacob.
Myth, Religion, and Mother Right: Selected Writings of J. J. Bachofen. Translated by Ralph Manheim. Bollingen Series, LXXXIV. Princeton: Princeton University Press, 1967. [Originally published in German, 1926.]

Bakan, David.
Disease, Pain, and Sacrifice: Toward a Psychology of Suffer-ing. Chicago: University of Chicago Press, 1968; Boston: Beacon Press, 1971.

Bakan, David.
The Duality of Human Existence: Isolation and Communion in Western Man. Chicago: Rand McNally, 1966; Boston: Beacon Press, 1971.

Bakan, David.
Sigmund Freud and the Jewish Mystical Tradition. With a new preface by the author. [1st ed. Princeton: Van Nostrand, 1958]; New York: Schocken Books, 1965; Boston: Beacon Press, 1975.

Bible.
The Anchor Bible. 52 vols. (projected). Garden City, New York: Doubleday, 1964–
   Vol. 1: *Genesis.* Introduction, translation, and notes by
      E. A. Speiser. 1964.
   Vol. 15: *Job.* Introduction, translation, and notes by
      Marvin H. Pope. 1965.
   Vols. 16–17A: *Psalms.* Introduction, translation, and notes
      by Mitchell Dahood. 3 vols. 1966–70.
   Vols. 29–29A: *John.* Introduction, translation, and notes
      by Raymond E. Brown. 2 vols. 1966–70.

Bible.
The New Oxford Annotated Bible: The Holy Bible, Revised Standard Version Containing the Old and New Testaments. Edited by Herbert G. May and Bruce M. Metzger. New York: Oxford University Press, 1973. [1st ed. 1962.]

Bible.
The Pentateuch and Rashi's Commentary. Translated by
Abraham Ben Isaiah and Benjamin Sharfman. 5 vols. Brook-
lyn, N.Y.: S. S. and R. Publishing Co., 1949.

Briffault, Robert.
*The Mothers: A Study of the Origins of Sentiments and In-
stitutions.* 3 vols. New York: Macmillan, 1927.

Campbell, Joseph.
The Masks of God: Primitive Mythology. Vol. 1 of 4 vols.
New York Viking Press, 1969. [1st ed. 1959.]

Cassirer, Ernst.
The Philosophy of Symbolic Forms. Translated by Ralph
Manheim. Preface and introduction by C. W. Herdel. 3 vols.
New Haven: Yale University Press, 1955–57. [Originally
published in German, 1923–29.]

Chesterton, Gilbert K.
Orthodoxy. London: John Lane, 1908. Reprinted Westport,
Conn.: Greenwood, 1974.

Chomsky, Noam.
*Cartesian Linguistics: A Chapter in the History of Rationalist
Thought.* New York: Harper and Row, 1966.

Cirlot, Juan Eduardo.
A Dictionary of Symbols. Translated from the Spanish by
Jack Sage. New York: Philosophical Library, 1962; 2nd ed.,
1972.

Cohen, Arthur A.
In the Days of Simon Stern: A Novel. New York: Random
House, 1973.

Daly, Mary.
Beyond God the Father: Toward a Philosophy of Women's Liberation. Boston: Beacon Press, 1973.

Daly, Mary.
The Church and the Second Sex. With a new feminist post-christian introduction by the author. New York: Harper and Row, 1975. [1st ed. 1968.]

Davis, Elizabeth G.
The First Sex. New York: G. P. Putnam's Sons, 1971.

Decter, Midge.
The New Chastity and Other Arguments Against Women's Liberation. New York: Coward, McCann and Geoghegan, 1972.

Descartes, René.
Meditations on First Philosophy. In *The Philosophical Works of Descartes.* Translated by Elizabeth S. Haldane and G. R. T. Ross. Corrected ed. 2 vols. Cambridge: Cambridge University Press, 1931. [1st. ed. 1911. Reprinted New York: Dover, 1955. Originally published in Latin, 1641.] Vol. 1, pp. 131–199.

Diner, Helen (pseudonym).
Mothers and Amazons: The First Feminine History of Culture. Edited and translated by John Philip Lundin, introduction by Brigitte Berger. Garden City, N.Y.: Doubleday, 1973. [1st ed. 1965. Originally published in German, 1932.]

Dodds, Eric R.
The Greeks and the Irrational. Berkeley: University of California Press, 1951.

Douglas, Mary.
Natural Symbols: Explorations in Cosmology. New York: Pantheon Books, 1970.

Douglas, Mary.
Purity and Danger: An Analysis of Concepts of Pollution and Taboo. Harmondsworth, England: Penguin Books, 1970. [1st ed. 1966.]

Eliade, Mircea.
Images and Symbols: Studies in Religious Symbolism. Translated by Philip Mairet. New York: Sheed and Ward, 1961. [Originally published in French, 1952.]

Eliade, Mircea.
The Myth of the Eternal Return; or, Cosmos and History. Translated by Willard R. Trask. 2nd printing, with corrections. Bollingen Series, XLVI. Princeton: Princeton University Press, 1965. [1st ed. 1954. Originally published in French, 1949.]

Eliade, Mircea.
The Sacred and the Profane: The Nature of Religion. Translated from the French by Willard R. Trask. New York: Harcourt, Brace, 1959. [Originally published in German, 1957.]

Eliade, Mircea.
The Two and the One. Translated by J. M. Cohen. New York: Harper and Row, 1965. [Originally published in French, 1962.]

Erigena, John Scotus.
Periphyseon: On the Division of Nature. Translated [from the Latin] by Myra L. Uhlfelder, with summaries by Jean A. Potter. Indianapolis: Bobbs-Merrill, 1976.

Frazer, James George.
The New Golden Bough. A new abridgement, edited and
with notes and foreword by Theodor H. Gaster. New York:
New American Library, 1964. [1st ed. 1959.]

Freud, Sigmund.
Beyond the Pleasure Principle. In *The Standard Edition of the
Complete Psychological Works of Sigmund Freud.* Trans-
lated under the general editorship of James Strachey. 24 vols.
London: Hogarth Press, 1953–74. Vol. 18, pp. 1–64. [Origi-
nally published in German, 1920.]

Freud, Sigmund.
Moses and Monotheism: Three Essays. Translated by James
Strachey. In *Complete Psychological Works.* Vol. 23, pp.
1–137. [Originally published in German, 1939.]

Freud, Sigmund.
"The Theme of the Three Caskets," translated by C. J. M.
Hubback, in *Complete Psychological Works.* Vol. 12, pp.
289–301. [Originally published in German, 1913.]

Fromm, Erich.
*The Forgotten Language: An Introduction to the Understand-
ing of Dreams, Fairy Tales and Myths.* New York: Rinehart,
1951.

Ginzberg, Louis.
Legends of the Bible. [Shorter version of *The Legends of the
Jews.*] Introduction by Shalom Spiegel. Philadelphia: Jewish
Publication Society of America, 1956.

Ginzberg, Louis.
The Legends of the Jews. 7 vols. Philadelphia: Jewish Publication Society of America, 1909–13.

11

111

Goethe, Johann Wolfgang von.
Faust. Translated with an introduction by Philip Wayne.
2 vols. Harmondsworth, England: Penguin Books, 1949–59.
[Originally published in German, 1790–1833.]

Gordon, Cyrus H.
The Common Background of Greek and Hebrew Civilizations.
2nd ed. New York: W. W. Norton, 1965. [1st ed. published
under title *Before the Bible*, 1962.]

Graves, Robert.
The White Goddess: A Historical Grammar of Poetic Myth.
Amended and enlarged ed. New York: Farrar, Straus and
Giroux, 1966. [1st ed. 1948.]

Graves, Robert, and Raphael Patai.
Hebrew Myths: The Book of Genesis. New York: Doubleday,
1964.

Gressmann, Hugo.
"Tod und Auferstehung des Osiris nach Festbräuchen und
Umzügen," in *Der Alte Orient*, vol. 23 (1923), no 3.

Harding, M. Esther.
*Woman's Mysteries, Ancient and Modern: A Psychological
Interpretation of the Feminine Principle as Portrayed in
Myth, Story, and Dreams*. New York: Bantam Books, 1973.
[1st ed. 1971.]

Harrelson, Walter.
From Fertility Cult to Worship. Garden City, N.Y.: Doubleday, 1969.

Harrison, Jane Ellen.
Mythology. New York: Harcourt, Brace and World, 1963.
[1st ed. 1924.]

Harrison, Jane Ellen.
Prolegomena to the Study of Greek Religion. 3rd ed. Cambridge: Cambridge University Press, 1922. [Reprinted New York: Meridian Press, 1955. 1st ed. 1903.]

Heilbrun, Carolyn G.
Toward a Recognition of Androgyny. New York: A. A. Knopf, 1973.

Heiler, Friedrich.
"The Madonna as a Religious Symbol," in *The Mystic Vision: Papers from the Eranos Yearbooks.* Translated by Ralph Manheim. Bollingen Series XXX, 6. Princeton: Princeton University Press, 1968. Pp. 348–374. [Originally published in German, 1934.]

Heschel, Abraham Joshua.
A Passion for Truth. New York: Farrar, Straus and Giroux, 1973.

Homeric Hymn to Demeter.
"The Homeric Hymn to Demeter," in *Hesiod, the Homeric Hymns and Homerica.* With an English translation by Hugh G. Evelyn-White. Loeb Classical Library, no. 57. Cambridge: Harvard University Press, 1914. Pp. 288–325.

Hooke, S. H.
Middle Eastern Mythology. Harmondsworth, England: Penguin Books, 1963.

Jung, Carl G.
"Archetypes and the Collective Unconscious," in *The Collected Works of Carl G. Jung.* Translated by R. F. C. Hull. Bollingen Series, XX. 19 vols. (projected) New York: Pantheon Books/Princeton: Princeton University Press, 1953–. Vol. 9, part 1, pp. 3–41. [Originally published in German, 1934.]

Jung, Carl G.
"The Concept of the Collective Unconscious," in *Collected Works.* Vol. 9, part 1, pp. 42–72. [Originally published in German, 1936–37.]

Kant, Immanuel.
Critique of Pure Reason. Translated by Norman Kemp Smith. New York: Macmillan, 1929. [Reprinted New York: St. Martin's Press, 1965. Originally published in German, 1781.]

Kerényi, C.
Eleusis: Archetypal Image of Mother and Daughter. Translated from the German by Ralph Manheim. Bollingen Series, LXV:4. New York: Pantheon Books, 1967. [Originally published in Dutch, 1960.]

Kerényi, C.
"The Mysteries of the Kabeiroi," in *The Mysteries: Papers from the Eranos Yearbooks.* Translated by Ralph Manheim. Bollingen Series, XXX, 2. New York: Pantheon Books, 1955. Pp. 32–63. [Originally published in German, 1945.]

Kierkegaard, Søren.
Fear and Trembling. In *Fear and Trembling, and The Sickness Unto Death.* Translated with introductions and notes by Walter Lowrie. Princeton: Princeton University Press, 1954. [1st ed. 1941. Originally published in Danish, 1843.]

Koepgen, Georg.
Die Gnosis des Christentums. Salzburg: O. Müller, 1939.

Kübler-Ross, Elisabeth.
On Death and Dying. New York: Macmillan, 1969.

Langer, Susanne K.
Mind: An Essay on Human Feeling. 2 vols. Baltimore: Johns Hopkins University Press, 1967–72.

Leach, Edmund.
"Genesis as Myth," in *Genesis as Myth, and Other Essays*.
London: Cape, 1969. Pp. 7–23.

Leach, Edmund.
"Lévi-Strauss in the Garden of Eden: An Examination of
Some Recent Developments in the Analysis of Myth," in
Transactions of the New York Academy of Sciences, vol. 23,
no. 4 (1961), pp. 386–396.

Lévi-Strauss, Claude.
*The Raw and the Cooked: Introduction to a Science of
Mythology, I.* Translated by John and Doreen Weightman.
New York: Harper and Row, 1969. [Originally published in
French, 1964.]

Lévi-Strauss, Claude.
"The Structural Study of Myth," in *Journal of American
Folklore*, vol. 68, no. 270 (Oct.–Dec. 1955), pp. 428–444.
[Reprinted as ch. 11 of his *Structural Anthropology*, 1963.]

Mayor, J. B.
"Mary (The Virgin)," in *A Dictionary of the Bible*. Edited by
James Hastings. 5 vols. New York: C. Scribner's Sons, 1898–
1904. Vol. 3, pp. 286–293.

Mechthild of Magdeburg.
*The Revelations of Mechthild of Magdeburg (1210–1297); or,
The Flowing Light of the Godhead.* Translated by Lucy
Menzies. London: Longmans, Green, 1953.

Mylonas, George E.
Eleusis and the Eleusinian Mysteries. Princeton: Princeton
University Press, 1961.

Neumann, Erich.
The Great Mother: An Analysis of the Archetype. Translated from the German by Ralph Manheim. 2nd ed. Bollingen Series, XLVII. Princeton: Princeton University Press, 1963. [1st ed. 1955.]

Nilsson, Martin P.
A History of Greek Religion. Translated by F. J. Fielden. 2nd ed. Oxford: Clarendon Press, 1949. [1st ed. 1925. Originally published in Swedish.]

Pallis, Marco.
"Is There a Problem of Evil?" in *Tomorrow,* vol. 11, no. 4 (Autumn 1963). [Reprinted in *The Sword of Gnosis: Metaphysics, Cosmology, Tradition, Symbolism,* edited by Jacob Needleman (Baltimore: Penguin Books, 1974), pp. 230–252.]

Patai, Raphael.
The Hebrew Goddess. New York: Ktav, 1967.

Piaget, Jean.
Genetic Epistemology. Translated from the French by Eleanor Duckworth. New York: Columbia University Press, 1970.

Piaget, Jean.
The Moral Judgment of the Child. Translated by Marjorie Gabain. New York: Free Press, 1965. [1st ed. and 1st ed. in French, 1932.]

Pines, Maya.
The Brain Changers: Scientists and the New Mind Control. New York: Harcourt Brace Jovanovich, 1973.

Plato.
Symposium. Translated by Michael Joyce. In *The Collected Dialogues of Plato.* Edited by Edith Hamilton and Huntington

Cairns. Bollingen Series, LXXI. New York: Pantheon Books, 1961. Pp. 526–574.

Plotinus.
The Enneads. Translated from the Greek by Stephen Mac-Kenna, revised by B. S. Page. 3rd ed. New York: Pantheon Books, 1962. [1st ed. 1955.]

Rank, Otto.
"The Myth of the Birth of the Hero," translated from the German by F. Robbins and Smith Ely Jelliffe, in *The Myth of the Birth of the Hero and Other Writings.* Edited by Philip Freund. New York: Vintage Books, 1959. Pp. 1–96.

Rashi (Solomon ben Isaac) *see* Bible. *The Pentateuch and Rashi's Commentary.*

Royce, Josiah.
"The Problem of Job," in *Studies of Good and Evil: A Series of Essays upon Problems of Philosophy and Life.* New York: D. Appleton, 1898. Pp. 1–28. [Reprinted in *Religion from Tolstoy to Camus,* edited by Walter Kaufmann (New York: Harper and Row, 1961), pp. 239–257.]

Salk, Lee.
"The Role of the Heartbeat in the Relations Between Mother and Infant," in *Scientific American,* vol. 228, no. 12 (May 1973), pp. 24–29.

Sartre, Jean-Paul.
Being and Nothingness: An Essay on Phenomenological Ontology. Translated and with an introduction by Hazel E. Barnes. New York: Philosophical Library, 1956. [Originally published in French, 1943.]

Sartre, Jean-Paul.
Existentialism. Translated by Bernard Frechtman. New York:
Philosophical Library, 1947. [Originally published in French,
1946.]

Scholem, Gershom G.
"Golem," in *Encyclopaedia Judaica: Das Judentum in
Geschichte und Gegenwart.* 10 vols. [A–Lyra; no more
published.] Berlin: Eschkol, 1928–34. Vol. 7, columns 501–507.

Scholem, Gershom G.
Major Trends in Jewish Mysticism. Translated [from the
German?] by George Lichtheim. 1st paperback ed. New York:
Schocken Books, 1961. [1st ed. 1941.]

Scholem, Gershom G.
On the Kabbalah and its Symbolism. Translated by Ralph
Manheim. New York: Schocken Books, 1965. [Originally
published in German, 1960.]

Scholem, Gershom G.
Sabbatai Sevi, the Mystical Messiah, 1626–1676. Translated
by R. J. Zwi Werblowsky. 2nd printing, with corrections.
Bollingen Series, XCIII. Princeton: Princeton University Press,
1975. [1st ed. 1973. Originally published in Hebrew, 1957.]

Shelley, Mary.
Frankenstein; or, The Modern Prometheus. With an afterword
by Harold Bloom. New York: New American Library, 1965.
[1st ed. 1816.]

Soloveitchik, Joseph B.
"The Lonely Man of Faith," in *Tradition,* vol. 7, no. 2
(Summer 1965), pp. 5–67.

Sophocles.
Oedipus at Colonus. In *Three Theban Plays: Antigone,
Oedipus the King, Oedipus at Colonus.* Translated by
Theodore Howard Banks. New York: Oxford University
Press, 1956. Pp. 85–133.

Spiegel, Shalom.
*The Last Trial; On the Legends and Lore of the Command
to Abraham to Offer Isaac as a Sacrifice: The Akedah.*
Translated by Judah Goldin. New York: Pantheon Books,
1967. [Originally published in Hebrew, 1950.]

Spinoza, Benedict de.
Ethic. Translated by W. Hale White, revised by A. H. Stirling.
4th ed. London: Milford, 1929. [1st ed. 1883. Originally
published in Latin, 1677.]

Straus, Erwin W.
"The Upright Posture," in *The Psychiatric Quarterly*, vol. 26
(1952), pp. 529–561. [Reprinted in *Phenomenological
Psychology: The Selected Papers of Erwin W. Straus,*
translated, in part, by Erling Eng (New York: Basic Books,
1966), pp. 137–165.]

Talmud.
Baba Bathra. Translated by Maurice Simon and Israel W.
Slotki. In *The Babylonian Talmud.* Edited by I. Epstein. 34
vols. London: Soncino Press, 1935–48. Section [4]: Nezikin,
vols. 3–4.

Tillich, Paul.
Dynamics of Faith. Edited by Ruth Nanda Anshen. New York:
Harper, 1957.

Tillich, Paul.
   On the Boundary: An Autobiographical Sketch. New York:
   C. Scribner's Sons, 1966. [Originally published as part 1 of
   The Interpretation of History, 1936.]

Weil, Simone.
   Waiting for God. Translated by Emma Craufurd. New York:
   Harper and Row, 1973. [1st ed. 1951. Originally published in
   French, 1950.]

Worringer, Wilhelm.
   *Abstraction and Empathy: A Contribution to the Psychology
   of Style.* Translated by Michael Bullock. New York: Interna-
   tional Universities Press, 1953. [Originally published in
   German, 1908.]

The Zohar. Translated by Harry Sperling, Maurice Simon, Paul
   P. Levertoff. 5 vols. London: Soncino Press, 1934. [Translation
   of the main body of the text, originally published in Aramaic,
   1558–60.]

INDEX